The Lost and Found and Other Stories

Elmer Holmes Bobst Awards for Emerging Writers

Established in 1983, the Elmer Holmes Bobst Awards in Arts and Letters are presented each year to individuals who have brought true distinction to the American literary scene. Recipients of the Awards include writers as varied as Toni Morrison, John Updike, Russell Baker, Eudora Welty, Edward Albee, Arthur Miller, Joyce Carol Oates, and James Merrill. The Awards were recently expanded to include categories devoted to emerging writers of poetry and fiction, and in 1993 the jurors selected winners in that category, Anne Marsella for her collection of short stories, *The Lost and Found and Other Stories,* and Stephan Torre for his collection of poetry, *Man Living on a Side Creek and Other Poems.*

ANNE MARSELLA

The
Lost and Found
and Other
Stories

NEW YORK UNIVERSITY PRESS
New York and London

NEW YORK UNIVERSITY PRESS
New York and London

Copyright © 1994 by New York University Press

Library of Congress Cataloging-in-Publication Data

Marsella, Anne.
The lost and found, and other stories / Anne Marsella.
p. cm.
Contents: Miss Carmen—The roommates—The lost and
found—Like father like son—Testimony—The blue suit
—My temple oh temple—The builder—The Mission San Mar-
tin—Fatiha's bells.
ISBN 0-8147-5502-X (cloth)—ISBN 0-8147-5503-8
(paperback)
I. Title.
PS3563.A7137L67   1994
813'.54—dc20   93-46128
                   CIP

New York University Press books are printed on acid-free paper,
and their binding materials are chosen for strength and durability.

Manufactured in the United States of America

10   9   8   7   6   5   4   3   2   1

Book design by Kathleen Szawiola

for Mom, Dad, and Joy

Contents

Acknowledgments

Special thanks to Sue Marson for her encouragement and insights and to M. Aiter for his help with Arabic.

The Lost and Found and Other Stories

Miss Carmen

*I*n Concepción, Chile, Carmen lived with her seven brothers and sisters. Sometimes she lived in the homes of her sisters, other times in the homes of her brothers. In the United States of America, in the Valley of San Joaquin she lived in guest bedrooms in the homes of wealthy matrons. In America, wherever she lodged, she had a colored television set. This was not so in Chile. She was middle aged, unmarried, had short, wavy gray hair as well as a silver-capped front tooth which she called the "beauty tooth." And then there was something one remarked about her cheeks when she smiled, perhaps that they were plum shaped and nothing more. Or else that they overwhelmed her mouth and gave her the look of a dizzy woman.

For a time, before leaving Chile, she had stayed with her brother, Jorge, who had begot three children, including an

3

exquisite daughter named Lupita, who had been crowned Little Miss Concepción at the age of four. Precious Lupita's hair had been dyed yellow for the competition but as Jorge's wife was a hairdresser this was carried off quite well. Carmen took meticulous care of the child's clothes, hand-washing them in delicate bleaches and ironing them. In truth she had been content at the house of Jorge, just as she had been at Juanita's and Carlos's and Pochi's and Victor's and Lima's, and Julio's. Only what is contentment to a willful dreamer? So little indeed. Certainly not enough. Carmen did not possess that arbitrarily extravagant je ne sais quoi common to the poetic soul. She wasn't a fantast in that way. Her dreams never exceeded her want but were a perfect echo of it. Never had she been falsified by a vision, by an unobtainable something. What can be said is that the recurrent image of herself propped on a Louis XIV fauteuil rested vivid in her mind's eye.

It was Carmen's cousin, Alberta, who had urged her to come to the Valley of San Joaquin. An affluent matriarch by the name of Mrs. J. M. Walker for whom Alberta polished silver, was looking for a live-in maid for part-time work. Alberta thought of Carmen who had always loved beautiful objects and the luxurious interiors of the homes in "Los Ricos y los Despiadados." She wrote in her letter, "Here the homes are the beautiful ones like those in 'The Rich and the Pitiless.' They can be cleaned with a pinkie. So there is very little work to do. And closets filled with fiesta shoes of the mistress. When she is gone you can put them on and iron this way. Here you will learn the names of things, things you have always wondered about. You will learn the names. And from the laundry you will know the private doings of the mistress and her mister. This would please you, would it not?"

Carmen thought about it. This proposition did appeal to her. She saw the hitherto-closed hand of opportunity open, offering its palm to her as a crossing bridge. Leading where? Ah! Carmen could not say. The salary was a handsome one too and she insisted on this as she would have a burden. Nevertheless she was somewhat apprehensive about leaving the milieu of loved ones, the familiar rituals, the concatenation of vowels. She thought of how they must speak in the Valley of San Joaquin and she feared it was something awful, ducklike, and exasperating.

For two weeks Carmen thought this proposition over. It sounded bad, it sounded good. She weighed it in her right hand, she weighed it in her left hand. Then, one Monday morning at ten o'clock, she walked down to the bus depot in a black and white checkered dress and bought a ticket. What made her do so? Perhaps she was swayed by a menopausal whim, or by the advice of a revenant. It would be hard to say. She announced her decision to leave that night at Jorge's dinner table. Jorge looked at her solemnly and held her by the shoulders with his arms outstretched. He said to her, "You are not my only sister, but you are my only sister who has cared for the clothes of my children. For this I will miss you." Her farewell was bid in a bon voyage party that lasted seven days, each of the seven siblings paying a day of tribute to their sister Carmen. When the festivities were exhausted, Carmen packed two suitcases and boarded the bus, the first of the many that would take her from Chile to the Valley of San Joaquin. Carmen's journey was a long and difficult one and is a story in itself. Let it be said that she arrived in the Valley of San Joaquin with a provisory black patch over her left eye. What had happened? She never told.

When Mrs. Walker showed Carmen her room, she looked from right to left and said in her language, "It will do." Had Mrs. Walker understood this, she would have been vexed. Carmen, however, did not say this to insult, nor was she being by any means discriminatory; she was simply concerned with what would do. She had never been a landlord and couldn't have understood the vanity of one. Her room was on the first floor and was furnished with a twin chintz covered bed, matching curtains and a love seat. There was also a small TV sitting on a commode. It should be said that Carmen was an ambitious woman in her own right. And if one were to ask how an aspiring woman could have concerned herself with the clothes of her brother's children, the wash and the wear of them, she would have said, "I have done this out of love." She could do one thing for love and be strongly desirous of another so very different. Clearly there were two hearts and two minds. She spoke to them in mismatched voices. Carmen was the sort of woman who could divide the family's pot of beans into sixteen equal servings. Nobody would feel cheated.

In the Valley of San Joaquin, she vividly saw what could be had and would not consider herself as a "have-not." Often she told Alberta, "The humans are divided into those who have and those who have-not; those who take and those who are taken. As this is true, I am one who takes and will have. This is prudence." When she saw the cumbrous jumbo television set in the billiard room, she resented Missie Walkie, as she called her, for her own insignificant one. Once, while she was dusting, she accidentally knocked the volume knob off the jumbo set. She pocketed it.

Mrs. Walker was happy enough with Carmen although she found her a few too many times sitting in an armchair when she should have been waxing or vacuuming. Mostly she had her cook and serve luncheons and dinner parties. For this Carmen was given a white doily to wear on her head and a matching apron. As she was awed by decorum and the wearing of uniforms, she found these occasions almost titillating. She smiled demurely at the guests. Her intention was to exhibit the beauty tooth and to seduce them. What this little trick got her was several jobs moonlighting outside the domain of Missie Walkie. For one there was Missie Smithie, president of the Junior League, who hired her to serve at her daughter's wedding reception. Carmen passed out dishes of relish on silver trays. Yes, she was quite skilled at this. She could walk up to anyone of any disposition and offer an hors d'oeuvre. Her latina gait, that slow, indolent sway of the hips was curious to some. It irritated and enticed in the same way as her smile. There was something puerile and almost sly about her, something that either coaxed a citizen of the Valley of San Joaquin or made him wary. She held out the tray and said, "You wantie?"

Carmen didn't pay taxes. She really was doing quite well and opened a savings account. She had easily procured more and more jobs for herself and could afford to refuse an offer if it reeked of the "difícil," as she said. Her speciality was catering. She loved the gala events. She abandoned Missie Walkie's doily for an oversized white bow that she clipped on the top of her head. She had a black mock evening gown, hemmed to knee length that she put on for catering. On her feet she wore white ballerina slippers. Shrewd as she was, Carmen managed to delegate the work to the "help" and arranged it so that her participation in the clean-ups was minimal. "Go do cakie," she might say. And the others would cut and serve the cake. "Washie dishie!" And the others would wash. It never occurred to Carmen that she couldn't speak English. She was understood. And she misunderstood when it was necessary.

After three years or so of industrious living in the Valley of San Joaquin, Carmen saw the many seeds she had sewn flower into nameable things, some of which she could wear, some of which she could tap. She had acquired much, including the jumbo set she had eyed and modestly vandalized in Missie Walkie's house. But there was one seed she had not thought of planting, perhaps because she knew how it could and had thrived, or because it had once been common enough to her. That one was the seed of the heart.

Time and again, Carmen had tried to entice her brothers and sisters to come settle in the Valley of San Joaquin with her. She had even made a down payment on a two-bedroom house for her brother Jorge and his wife and children. But Jorge was kept in Chile by several dubious mining investments. The others all had one excuse or another not to join her. Carmen eventually gave up on the idea altogether and for a while was angry and sent vindictive letters, boasting of her successes and threatening to disown them. But had she ever owned them? She asked herself this and felt merciless, as if she tread alone in a world without mercy. Grace! When was the last time she had felt the luminosity of it in her body? Hope? Things sufficed and the jaded soul didn't search it. Charity? She fed the pigeons! Carmen was not a woman to plead, "I'm lonely in the Valley of San Joaquin." Such a confession would either have cured or worsened her spiritual disarray. She took a middle ground instead and was childishly bilious. She overpeppered luncheon consommés and mistreated ladylike palates. She loaded the dishwasher with crystal. Missie Walkie suffered the losses. Carmen was cavalier and ornery with the peerage. On Thanksgiving she stuffed Missie Walkie's turkey with a fiery mole filling. The family was aghast although some were proud and feebleminded enough to eat it. Only to be all the more miserable with gastric fever the following day. After this, Missie Walkie dismissed Carmen, giving her three days to prepare her departure. She could not forgive the nimiety of blunders and Carmen offered no apologies.

Carmen was proud but she was also a taker. Her pride then, was merely a convenient peccadillo, a vanity that kept her on the desirous side of humanity. It in no way hindered her propensity to help herself. Nor did the rift with Mrs. Walker preclude her from finding another refuge in the milieu. Carmen had someone in mind when she left, the widow of a ranchero tycoon from Spain, Señora Valdéz. Señora Valdéz herself was not Spanish, she was from a Southern state and emigrated to the Valley of San Joaquin as the result of a dust storm. She met the Señor Valdéz at the Raisin Ball and made a fruitful marriage. She needed someone to "do vegetables and linens" as she put it, and on several occasions had offered Carmen her guest house in exchange for kitchen help. Carmen did not call her up, as she never used the phone, but walked there. She lived seven blocks down from Mrs. Walker on the same street. It was an easy walk for a robust woman like Carmen and when she got to the house of Señora Valdéz, there were some twenty cars parked around it. Señora Valdéz was entertaining. Carmen was intent on her predicament and didn't hesitate to walk through the gate and into the backyard where the cocktail party was in full swing. Señora Valdéz, a flamboyant blond with an imperious nose, was holding a highball and laughing, her head thrown back. Surrounding her were several dashing gentlemen looking bemused in summer suits. Although Carmen spotted her straight off, she made a stop at the hors d'oeuvre table first. She was famished. After having a few bites, she walked up to Señora Valdéz from behind and tapped her on the shoulder. The woman reeled around and saw her there with the white bow on her head.

"It's Missie Carmie!" she let out for the others' amusement. The woman was lit. Then calming a bit, but with the same condescending tone she asked her, "Carmen, what can we do for you? Or are you here for the party?"

Carmen ignored this mockery and kept to what she knew best, not self-righteousness but seduction. She smiled coyly at Señora Valdéz and bared the beauty tooth.

"Missie Carmie not at casa Missie Walkie more. She do kitchen for Señora and live in house?"

"Oh God, the vegetables. That's right. Got to have someone do the vegetables. You know, that Costa Rican girl I had just left last month . . . Left with the neighbor's gardener! She told me he had had his stomach tied. You know, he was fat. F-A-T! I said to her, 'Juanita, if those tubes come untied you got yourself a lard ass.' But she left with him. I just got a letter from her in Mexico. She was such a sweet thing. And you know, she just loved me. She kept herself so clean. So clean!"

She took another sip of her highball and narrowed in on Carmen, a bit too severely, as was her way.

"OK Carmen, but you know how I like them done." And here she demonstrated with her hands, as if pulling threads. "Julienne, like they do in Paris. Julienne!"

Then an expansive woman in a green mousseline dress appeared and took Señora Valdéz by the arm claiming that she hadn't seen her in ages. Carmen left and went into the kitchen where a heavy-legged woman named Fanny was slowly decorating a platter of Armenian delicacies. Carmen swiftly took the platter from her and went back out to the garden. She wove her way through the guests, serving and seducing them, not with her sex appeal, for this she took to heart and saved for her people, but with her quaintness, her bow and her accent. Those were her gimcracks and she arranged them most successfully. Late that night when the company finally left, Señora Valdéz, in her après soirée stupor, handed Carmen the keys to the guest house. Carmen found the bed and slept until ten o'clock the next day.

Working for Señora Valdéz suited Carmen as it was essentially a morning job and left her afternoons free for going to the shopping malls or watching soap operas. Señora however, was a difficult, exigent woman who impatiently repeated herself and demanded perfection from her entourage. She was a Catholic though, unlike the other matrons for whom Carmen had worked. At least she wouldn't have to think of her as a heretic. Every Sunday Señora took Carmen to mass with her at Our Lady of Victory. Carmen usually would take the bus home from the church as she liked to stay after and play bingo with the Las Mujeres del Salvador guild. She never risked befriending anybody in the group. She was afraid she might be asked for something. Carmen was fundamentally clannish. Had one of the women been from the same village as she, then perhaps she would have extended a hand and opened her breast in intimacy. But then again maybe not. For Carmen there had always been family and others, never a friend, never a foe. Her relation to either group went unquestioned, to one she was inextricably joined by blood and obligation and the other she observed indifferently, like the cat that sniffs at his dinner only to walk away and then come back later to nibble disdainfully at it. Carmen fed off others and with a sense of duty, which for her was love, fed family and family only.

The most wonderful thing about the house of Señora Valdéz was, to Carmen's mind, the opulent selection of arm chairs in the formal living room. One of them was a faux Louis XIV so like the one she had envisioned for many years. "Yes," she thought to herself, "It is this one." How stunning it was, how ravishingly fine in every way. Carmen was benumbed at the sight of it. She was overwhelmed by the beauty of the object, by the rich persimmon color of its upholstery. The chair itself sat in a posture so ingeniously conceived. It sat, formidable and beckoning in a corner of the elegant salon. For weeks Carmen would go into the living room to gaze at it. Everything about it was sublime and as she looked at it, both ardor and despair welled in her. She moaned. And pulled at her pantyhose. And hugged herself as if protecting a child at the breast.

It so happened that one evening Señora Valdéz asked Carmen to stay in the house while she was gone. She was going to a gala at the country club and as her neighbor had just been robbed the previous night she was worried about leaving the house empty. Carmen agreed to do this. Señora Valdéz had four TVs and an ice box filled with Belgian chocolates and French pastries. So Carmen took her knitting with her into the house, bid Señora good-bye and locked the doors behind her. She sat in the kitchen for a time and watched the channel vente-uno news. She helped herself to soda pops and chocolates. Then she decided she needed to go to the bathroom. She just loved the bathrooms of Señora Valdéz which were plush with floor-to-ceiling mirrors, marble counter tops and gold faucets. They were very different from those sober ones in Missie Walkie's house. This was because Señora was a Catholic and the other was not. That was how Carmen saw it. To get to the bathroom she had to pass through the living room and it was in doing so that she was stopped short in her tracks. In fact nothing impeded her physically from going on. Yet there was an incandescent stillness in the room that defied a trespasser, that belittled the need to get from one point to another, a silence that said of itself to the intruder, "Silencio, Por favor!" It was as if the dim light of the room were issued from a singular dream-hole.

And as if this dream-hole had been carved above the objet d'art to illuminate it. The rest of the room was left in the glow of its wake. It was a brazen jewel the color of a stone unheard of and never seen. Carmen's mouth watered. It was a fruit of ecstatic flavors unknown to the tongue. She craved and ached for it. Carmen stood in the middle of the room, her eyes riveted upon the fauteuil. But it was not her eyes that perceived the chair's beckoning. What registered this were the cords of her body, her yearning instinct. Carmen went to the armchair, solemnly with her head tilted upward and sat upon it transfixed. And at once she fell into a reverie so vivid and fiery, a reverie of carnal delights and dignity balls, of sumptuous banquets and courtesans. She dreamed of what was wicked and splendid, here of the sublime, there of the abject. It was an amalgam of slothful postures and pristine comportments. Did she want all this? God knows. Carmen surpassed herself. For the first time in her life perhaps, she surpassed herself.

As it turned out, Señora was a good deal deaf and asked Carmen to answer the phone when she was in the house doing vegetables and linens. This didn't please her a bit and when she answered she said, "Hola." She was curt on the phone. Some days she unplugged all of Señora's phones for her own peace of mind. Usually Señora didn't notice. She spent her mornings in the beauty shop in any case. The voices on the line were always the same to Carmen. They were nagging ones, asking things of her she found unbecoming and didn't care to understand. One day however, when she answered the phone, the voice she heard was not a Valley of San Joaquin voice but one kindred to her own. It was a man and she immediately addressed him in Spanish.

"If you want the Señora Valdéz, she is not here. If you know her then you know that she is at the beauty shop every morning until twelve. At twelve she comes home and has the dietetic lunch which I weigh on the scale for her. Then she naps until three. She does not take calls before three. She doesn't call back so you needn't leave a message." Carmen was able to say what she had wanted to say many a time and this was a great relief to her.

"Tell her that the foreman of the ranch has called. She knows me by the first name. I am Manuel, the ranch foreman. Tell her that I will be by at four o'clock with five legs of lamb, bread that I baked in the ground and six crates of seedless grapes. There is business I must do with her."

"I will tell her this."

But Carmen forgot to tell Señora and when the foreman drove up in his truck, the woman was still in her nap-time negligé. Carmen was sent out to stall him until the other could make herself decent. Manuel was a heavyset man, florid in the face and with a square Spanish brow. He had several boxes of grapes in his arms when Carmen greeted him. She had her bow on top of her head and had put on a scoop neck sundress that flatteringly revealed her embonpoint.

"Hello," she said through the beauty tooth. "You can set those down in the kitchen. Come this way." She led him through several gates and then through the back door into the kitchen. The man put them down on a counter with a grunt and went back out to get the rest of what he had brought. Carmen followed him.

"I would help you but I am not meant to carry heavy things. I am not a housekeeper who pushes vacuums and overturns sofas. I do vegetables and linens only. I live in the guest house next to the pool. Where do you live?" Carmen watched his back as he lifted the heavy burlap sacks of lamb out of the truck. She watched the strength of his arms and his back and his squatty legs as he swiftly delivered his goods, one and then the next into the kitchen. She watched him intently and pondered. He reminded her of something, something she hadn't seen in many years it seemed. Yes, he reminded her of a man. He was a man! She was giddy. Had things become such that she had forgotten? What about all those men she served finger foods to at the galas? Clearly they were different from this one. They were another something. This manual laborer, this Manuel clad in ranchero wear was a man, like those she had left behind her in Las Pampas. Carmen shuddered.

"I live in the foreman's house on a hill above the ranch. It has two bathrooms and two bedrooms. There is a living room with a very big window. It gives onto the Valley of San Joaquin like you have never seen her before. She is not a greedy valley but she is a mean one."

Carmen said no more. Nor did he. Señora Valdéz walked in and effusively greeted the foreman, kissing him on both cheeks as she had seen her late husband's people do. He was a simple man as they say and this sort of theatrics embarrassed him. His face turned almost purple.

Carmen quietly left them and went back to the guest house. There she laid down on her back and thought of the man.

What Señora and Manuel spoke of in part, was Señora's own garden. She asked Manuel to pick the grapes that hung ripe and abundantly from her trellis. The birds were making a mess of them and she needed it taken care of right away. She also asked him to pick the peach trees of which there were six. Manuel agreed to do so the following week. Carmen was in the kitchen cleaning leeks when she saw him through the window walking into the backyard with burlap and canvas paraphernalia and cutters in hand. Then he went into the toolshed and brought out a ladder, setting it underneath the vineyard trellis. He began clipping off the grapes. For several hours she watched him as she cleaned, peeled, sliced, and diced. She imagined herself the fruit in his hands, in the hands of Manuel. She saw that they were strong and had held much of life. They were indiscriminate hands and for this Carmen wanted to kiss them. Because such hands were the finest but were never the rewarded. They were hardly loved appropriately. It was a scorchingly hot day but Manuel did not take off his shirt. He was in the garden of an Anglo-Saxon and didn't forget this.

When the Señora came home, she waved hello to Manuel and proceeded into the kitchen for the dietetic lunch. She asked Carmen to make some sandwiches for Manuel. Carmen made a copious lunch platter for him with two roast beef sandwiches, potato salad, three-bean salad, corn on the cob, and chips. For dessert she would later give

him a fudgesicle. She also gave him two beers and a sparkling water. She set all this on a tray and carried it out
to him.

"Lunch!" she called out.

Manuel looked up a bit stunned, as a man who forgets
his hunger in work until he is reminded of it, and came
down from the ladder. Carmen set the tray down on the
table and waited. Manuel took off the burlap bags heavy
with grapes he had been wearing and wiped his hands
with a handkerchief. Then he sat down to eat. He looked
briefly at Carmen and said, "Gracias," nodding his head.
Carmen took this as an invitation to sit down at the table.
Manuel was very hungry indeed and ate greedily. Carmen
thought of the roastbeef sandwiches she made, she had put
horseradish on them and was glad at that moment for
having done so. "He is a caballero," she said to herself.
She could see that he took pleasure in eating, like a wolf,
and did not speak to him. Carmen watched him and had
he not had such an appetite he might have noticed this. As
it was, he was seemingly unaware of her presence or at
least undisturbed by it. When he was at last finished, he
pushed the tray away from him and sat back in his chair.
He rested his hands on his belly. And began to speak,
perhaps to Carmen but most likely not.

"A man can live alone with sheep and vineyards for
many years and then one day it will not be enough. He
can build his own house with the fruit of his labors and
this will not be enough. A man can invent a machine and
this too, will not be enough."

"Yes," said Carmen, although she didn't understand
him really.

"A man," he went on, "wears pants, a shirt, suspenders, and shoes. A caballero wears a hat. Still this is not enough. A man is judged on these things that are not enough. They are nothing. There are very few honest men. But even an honest man is not enough."

Carmen was beginning to fathom his words and wanted to say to him, "I am enough! I am!" She wanted to assuage that misery in him, the sadness that made him say that all he was and had was not enough. She wondered how he could say such things when everything was at his feet, when everything that was, was enough. It was! And she was there, his angel of mercy. "See me! see me!" she wanted to cry out. "For the love of you I am enough!" But Manuel didn't see her. He stood back up, loaded himself with burlap sacks and climbed the ladder.

Manuel came three more times that week and each time Carmen fixed him a lunch and watched him eat it. And after each lunch he would lean back and speak of regret and sorrow in a way that excluded Carmen, that fixed her as a voiceless listener. How she wanted to say, "You are missing me! Missing me while I sit in front of you." But could not. His way tied her throat in a knot. It was only at night under that same trellis that the knot worked itself free and Carmen was given to monologues so tiresome, so depleting that several times she finished the evening curled up under a peach tree.

After Manuel finished his work at Señora's there was no sign of him, although Carmen longed desperately for one. She no longer unplugged the phone but nervously picked it up when it rang hoping to hear his voice on the line. Often she pictured him in front of the big window he had spoken of looking out at the Valley of San Joaquin which was mean and beautiful but not enough and she wept for his sorrow, which was hers. That was enough for her. Perhaps the only respite she had from her pining was the fauteuil. The armchair had become for her not simply an object, but a phenomenon and a haven. She sat in it once or twice a day, careful to know the whereabouts of the Señora when she did so. And in the chair she gave herself up to the most delicious of reveries, sometimes elaborately baroque, other times serene and windless.

It was true that there were days more hope filled than others for Carmen. On these more inspired mornings she arose from bed with the good faith that there would be news of her beloved. She took a naive pleasure in such mornings but was left by the end of the day in a state of utter want, all the more desperate and dispirited. Carmen frequented the armchair often and usually at one o'clock when the Señora spoke on the kitchen phone with her best friend, Trudy. It was in the month of October, two months after Manuel had left and not come back that, while sitting in the Louis XIV, she had a fleeting vision. In this vision she was wrapped in scarlet drapes and carried by birds through the sky. She was being taken back to her homeland, to the alluvial plains of Bio-Bio. Everything appeared so quaint below her, she laughed. Her laughter sounded like tinkling bells. The birds brought her to a green mountain, one she had seen in her childhood. Only it had been carved into a castle. The birds left her at the door of it and she stood there regally for a moment, draped in crimson. Then Carmen came back to herself and to the room and felt the chair under her hams. The vision had left her more awake than she had been in months. Her senses were frighteningly keen. She could smell the rose bouquet from the back bedroom and her eyesight was so sharp she noticed a minute whiskey stain on the carpet that even the impeccable Señora had not spotted. But she was most stunned by her ears which registered clearly the phone conversation in the kitchen and by her crisp mind which effortlessly understood every word of that language she had grown so weary of and no longer bothered to listen to.

"No, Saturday is out. I've got that damned wedding to go to. You know, the foreman's getting married. Manuel ... That's right. I was out at the ranch yesterday. I gave him a little bonus, you know. And he says to me, 'Señora Valdéz, it would be an honor if you would be our witness.' So I'm in for the whole works. He's got himself a picture bride from Mexico. She gets here Friday and the wedding's Saturday. Olay! Oh my Gawd! He showed me her picture. Real excited about it, you know. She's got a round face like they do but she's pretty enough now. Just wait though. I tell you, in a few years she'll be F-A-T like the rest of them. I mean F-A-T! ..."

Carmen picked herself up, untied her apron, and went out the back door. It was hot in the Valley of San Joaquin. Even in October it was hot. It was a desert in fact. As Carmen walked down the street, her white ballerina slippers turned gray with dust.

The Roommates

There are streets in Paris where the tourist seeking thrill and knapsack curio does not venture, unless of course he makes an ill-advised right- or left-hand turn, whichever it may be, and finds himself inauspiciously there, feeling suddenly as if his pants were too tight or his pockets too swollen for the occasion. And he will lament the mishap and fumble through his guidebook to orient his whereabouts. But his map may not avail him for such streets are considered hardly worth indicating for the likes of him, they are too narrow and dark, and offer him nothing but offscourings and brouhaha. And so he makes his way through them, sullenly, until he spots the gates of the city, the truer one, the City of Offerings. The rues St. Timothé and Casimir du Loup expressed no readiness to give what the visitor might care to see or to touch, although the drab buildings along them welcomed the committed immigrants with open doors and coveted work permits. Along these streets and others like them, were sweatshops, stacked on top of each other some four or five stories high. And into these shops came the People of the World; the deracinated seekers, the beauties and the beasts. They came to this city perhaps because of despair or because of lust. In any case they came to live but instead they worked, so miserably some that they could not even muster to say to themselves, "Ah but today I am unhappy. It is this work that is breaking me." This leisure of thought which the tourist exploits so casually many of them may not possess.

Mary and Selma worked in sweatshop number twenty-seven on the rue Casimir du Loup. Mary sewed and Selma pressed. Neither envied what the other did. Both were content and overwhelmed in their proper tasks. They arrived nearly at the same time in Paris and at sweatshop number twenty-seven, Selma a bit before Mary, and took to each other straight away. There were few young women there and they sought each other out for companionship. Both were delighted. Mary was an African girl from Kenya and her arrival in France was, unlike Selma's, an error. She was, in fact, due to go to the United States of America, where her fiancé, Wilbur, was expecting her. And she had so longed to go there, to "that clever place," as she called it, not only to reunite with her love but also to have the pleasures of so many dresses and hairdos and cleaning products. Mary loved to clean and to polish, to wax and to mop. She also liked to peel potatoes as she had been taught at the Roman school. That is to say, with a paring knife.

On the day of her departure she was accompanied by

her mother and father who were so afraid of her missing her boat that they simply rushed her onto the first departing one they came to at the port. It was the wrong boat. And so when Mary finally glimpsed shore, it was not the torch-bearing virago that she had been expecting to see that she saw, but the blanched cliffs of Marseilles instead. "I think I make a terrible mistake," she said to herself, "It is the big white lady I must see not all these boats and cliffs and big clay houses." But she was ushered off the boat with the others and left alone on the docks where she wept, bitter with despair.

Mary was quite a big girl with lanky arms and legs and a beautiful head the shape of a sparrow's egg. Her face was serious but kind and not given to any great flux of expression. As she roamed with her mother's imperious stride which she borrowed for her trip, she drew attention to herself for she was a lovely sprig of a something, a fresh and edible something. Her gaze was as candid as that of a doe. Sailors, as she walked by them, made their lewd propositions and held out their hands beckoningly toward her. She said to them, "I have no alms for you. I am a poor girl and lost in this fiendish city." These words reminded her that she was not with dear Wilbur in the United States of America and she cried over the sadness of this. Still, she lacked the means to get to her lover and eventually decided to make her way to Paris which she had heard was a great city of opportunity, to find work. She was offered a ride there by an immigrant trucker from Gabon. He was transporting Roman tomatoes and got them to Paris in six hours. He dropped her off on the rue St. Timothé and she managed as she could from there.

Selma came to Paris by straightforward means; she took the eighty-six-hour bus from Istanbul. When she arrived in Paris she went to an inexpensive, one-star hotel that had been recommended to her. This hotel was on the rue Casimir du Loup, and was as grimy and as rapacious as the neighboring sweat-shops, although Selma did not notice this right away as she had arrived late at night. When she woke up to her first morning in Paris, she stretched her arms out above her and said, "Lord be with me." For she was beginning a new day and did not know what it would bring. She dressed in a burnt-colored sundress which fit snuggly around her hips and bosom and brushed her long, ratty, hennaed hair. Selma had the kind of body that smelled and felt and looked like a body. She couldn't help herself. Such purely sensual women as she, often have difficult and assumptive lives. This is not to say that they are arrogant but rather that the sensual woman will have many instant successes and assume too hastily that the instant is meant to be prolonged. How long can any man keep a woman who is entirely of the senses? Not very long she finds. So she develops a stamina both headstrong and aloof for matters of the heart. Because a woman must keep on after all. Selma was not an exception to her kind in any way. She was not the slightest bit exceptional and was much less beautiful than she reckoned herself to be. But how smart of her really. This view of herself gave her the assurance of a beautiful woman and so she appeared to others as lovely although she was not. She had a penchant for sportsmen because of the blessed feel of them and ached for their aches, and hungered for their hungers. She only knew how to feel a man and not how to own one. So she was left behind time and again and often with a jejune scar or tattoo of sorts on her bum, the mark of some javelin trainee or free-style swimmer.

Once Selma had finished her rather hasty toilette that morning, she went downstairs for her continental breakfast. However, seeing that coffee and rolls were served at one long table which was already filled by gruff men in blue overalls, she continued on and left the hotel. She stepped out onto the rue Casimir du Loup, too hopeful yet to guess that this street was to traffic her destiny as it had that of many others, that it would trade her dreams in so cavalierly for a modicum of infrequent delights, a cantaloupe, in winter, say, or a thin slice of salmon during the Rogation Days. Selma could not have known this then, as she walked along the sidewalk, her hips swaying as they did. All she could think was, "I am now in this city of Paris." It was a singular thought and offered her protection. The words took wings and became the guardian angel above her shoulder. It was indeed, she felt, a blessed morning. Trucks loading and unloading goods made great commotion and their tramontane drivers sent appreciative whistles her way. This pleased her and she said to herself, "These men want to ravish me. I am ravishing." And she kept on her path, paying no attention to the men despite her desire, perhaps to please them with her hands, until she came to number twenty-seven where she was stopped. Someone was pulling at her arm. It was a heavyset Greek with a wide, tough, goatlike head. This was Mr. Fred, the sweatshop foreman.

"Where are you going so fast?" he asked her with a surly smile. "You look like a hungry girl. Come with me

29

and I will feed you a thing or two." Still holding onto her arm he opened the door to the sweatshop and pulled her in. There was a great industrious din in the place as they walked past many women hunched over sewing machines. Soon they came to a red, painted door in the back. Mr. Fred unlocked it with a key and they went in. It was a small room with a wooden chair, a table, and a filing cabinet. He offered her a seat and fed her some crackers and cheese and olives. Selma really was famished and she ate quickly what he gave her. Then she thanked him.

"Thank you very much, for you have shown me that this city of Paris is a very hospitable one. I am happy to know this. Thank you."

"Ah! So you are new here then. You have not been here long at all!" Mr. Fred said this although he had know all along of course that she was a nouvelle-arrivée, and very freshly arrived at that. But this was a game he enjoyed and he would play it.

"No. I arrived last night on the eighty-six-hour bus from Istanbul. This is my first morning in Paris. I will now look for work so that I may soon take a flat, like the smart Parisian working girls."

"Ah! You fortunate girl. Do you know that your luck is very good today? Do not look any farther. There is no need. Here, in my shop I have a job for you. It's a very sweet job and the pay is more than fine for such a girl as you. How do you think of this?"

"This is wonderful to hear. I thank you again and again." Mr. Fred, who did indeed not only expect gratitude but a specific expression of it, pulled her to him and gave her pleasure. This was how, in Selma's first day in Paris, she procured for herself both a lover and a job.

After a month of working at the pressing machines, Selma, with the help of Mr. Fred, had enough money to rent a one-room flat on the fifth floor of the sweatshop twenty-seven building. It was a rather dark room with rose-print wallpaper and was furnished modestly with a large double bed and an overstuffed sofa the color of greenbeans. There was also a makeshift kitchen in one corner with a small refrigerator, a hot plate, a sink, and a radio. Selma was quite delighted with her flat, especially with its very wide bed where she made love with Mr. Fred. She had never seen a bed quite like it before and she was happy to be in Paris where such beds could be found. She kept a chamber pot beneath it. The WC was on the *palier*.

When the two women, Selma and Mary befriended each other, they often spent their evenings in the one-room flat, visiting. And eventually, seeing that Mary was staying in a squalid hotel and hoping to move from there, Selma suggested that she join her in sharing the flat. Mary agreed and moved in immediately with a suitcase and a cosmetics trunk. It was very economical for both of them. What Selma had not bothered to consider before making this suggestion to Mary, because indeed it did not bother her, were the nightly visits of the foreman, Mr. Fred. Selma was not concerned with pudency, perhaps because she had not been told what it was. That everyone knew that she was the casual concubine of the foreman did not disturb her in the least then. Her own sense of self went so unquestioned she would have been at pains to wonder at the notions of others. She was in truth a bore, but a comely and warm-hearted one.

The girls were quite pleased with their arrangement and celebrated the evening Mary moved in with a bottle of sparkling wine. They turned on the radio and danced. Mary, dancing the dances of the Motherland, moved her hips so furiously and with such abandon that her friend thought to herself, "Perhaps she is much like me. And enjoys what I enjoy as much as I enjoy it." They turned the radio up very loud and flung each other about laughing and gyrating. Then there was a knock on the door. Mary turned down the radio box and Selma went to answer the door. It was Mr. Fred. He barreled in with a bottle of spirits in his hand and slapped Selma playfully on the fanny, that region of hers that had always received the most attention and handling. Drinks were poured and the music was turned back up. Mr. Fred grabbed Selma around the waist and danced with her closely so that his groin pressed into hers. He grunted a bit while the girl threw her head back and bellowed with pleasure. They danced like this for a time, stopping for a drink here and there. But always dancing in this frenzied way, arousing each other so that there was no question as to where their pas de deux would end. Indeed they eventually tumbled upon the amatory bed and engaged in the most exigent of lovemaking.

During this time, Mary was seated on the sofa where she had retreated almost the moment Mr. Fred entered the flat. She was dismayed that her boss had come and put an end to her enjoyment of the party. She had been feeling the cords of her body coming to life once again with the dancing after a long day at the industrial sewing machine. Oh but he was a killjoy that brute! She could almost detest him but seeing that her dear friend felt differently toward him, she simply sat, without a thought and watched. Or maybe she did harbor thoughts yet she sat quietly throughout, like a cat that watches its master take a lover to bed. A cat will sit so still with its gaze fixed on the lovers, a gaze that would set them ill at ease if they took notice of it. For who might know what the cat is thinking? What is its knowledge and judgment? The cat will see what the lovers do not. Mary never spoke of what she saw. And when Selma made confidences about her affair with the foreman, Mary did not conspire with her as women often do. She did not enter into that feminine secrecy. For her there was none. Again and again she had been made a witness. When Selma spoke of her romantic trifles and begged the other's empathy, Mary only made obtuse and cursory remarks, which disappointed her friend. She did not care to embrangle herself in something that was not hers. She was in no way spiteful or emulous, and Selma knew better than to think of her in this light. She could bare her soul to her friend, but she could not expect her to engage in the expressions of intimacy. Mary could only be intimate in quiet, tidy ways; perhaps only in her personal hygiene.

Mr. Fred came to the girls' apartment four or five evenings a week for his ritualized visits. There was hardly ever a recess. He was a most assiduous man. Although there was little calculation or mechanics to their lovemaking, there was in fact, a prescribed order to it, an order which Mary could easily have outlined in a notebook but which the lovers themselves could not have. How ignorant they were of their own coupling! But they were yet spontaneous and fumbling and clever in pleasing. And for this reason, Mary's attention was still held. On these nights she would keep her vigil on the couch hearing the swoons and watching the rocking bodies. It was very cold alone on the couch and she slept as she could without a blanket. She hugged her knees and spoke to them as she would have a playmate. For several months she slept in this way but with the advent of winter she found it more and more difficult to find solace from the cold of her sleeping place. Then one night, still awake, she watched the lovers sleeping complacently. They each snored in their proper rhythms. Selma muttered a bit. Mr. Fred passed wind from time to time. A gelid chill like a running flagellum lashed at Mary's heart so that she put her hand to her chest to stop the shudder. And the vision came to her then, of the Bleeding Heart and of the sanguine rains of the Romans. She thought of the flesh, that of the others first, then of her own. Mary said to herself, "I am too cold to sleep. That is a very big bed we have there. I will go and climb in on the left-hand side. So that I may sleep in the warmth of blankets and bodies." She snuck into the bed without making a noise and fell into a heavy slumber.

The following morning, Selma was the first to awaken and she woke up to a sight that took her breath from her. There beside her was Mr. Fred sleeping with his head on Mary's breast, his arm flung around her. She took note of this and regained her wind. "Yes, now I see how it is. She has invited herself into the bed and it is in the bed that she is finally noticed." It was true that Mr. Fred had never paid attention to Mary. She had been part of a quotidian scenery at the shop and at the one-room flat. Yet in the course of one night this had changed. Mary had crept from the couch and was now in the hub. "Hoy!" Selma seemed to hear her call out, "I, too, can drive the beasts of Man!" And she was certain that Mary could. Selma was forlorn that morning and dressed without vibrato while the new pair, fresh with their discovery, were waking up. This is not to say that she was lamenting a loss but rather that she was adjusting to a change in habits. Her pelvic bones were aching and she knew that they also were re-fashioning themselves to accommodate the times. This was a bit difficult for her as she truly had been taken by surprise. Her flagrant indiscretion had kept her from foreseeing it. She simply had no sense of propriety.

And so it went that Mr. Fred continued to come four or five nights a week with a bottle of spirits as before, only he danced and bedded now, with the Kenyan girl. Selma was for a time, the odd woman out, sitting on the couch hardly entertained yet hardly bored. She smoked her Turkish cigars voraciously. She puffed and puffed and sat in her cloud of smoke. She was not catlike, intent and still as Mary had been on the couch but adopted another feline posture, that of a sensuous sprawl. And one night then, while she listened to the writhing couple, she was moved to touch herself. She did so and moaned with the pleasure of it. And shook the sofa. Hearing her from the bed, Mr. Fred must have remembered the longing he had had for her, the longing he had put aside for the other girl, perhaps he even felt that he missed her, for he rose from the big bed and went over to her.

The next morning, both women knew that another change had come about, one that might even be more livable and sustainable. But it was hard to tell exactly. Each adapted as she could. Selma bought herself a shiny red vinyl purse from a wholesale shop on the rue St. Timothé. Mary spent her Saturday afternoon in the beauty shop at Château d'Eau getting her hair extended. The girls went to see a movie together Saturday night. They saw *A Bout de Souffle*. Neither one of them cared much for it. But they left the theater arm in arm and went into various cafés for drinks, always standing at the counter and not sitting at tables as the French ladies did. They drank quite a bit and were soon giggling together at the circus of bodies around them, at the mustache of one and at the tiny foot of another. Suddenly Selma burst out with a thick tongue, "Mr. Fred loves my bottom. He says that it is like the heavenly cushion upon which the Lord sits."

"Ah yes?" said her friend, "And this Mr. Fred loves very much my breasts. He says to me, 'These are the dark plumbs of God. Happy is the man who tastes their sweetness.' "

At this both women roared, Selma with her head thrown back, Mary with tears in her eyes. And when their eyes met, they laughed and laughed again. Selma slapped her hand on the counter and tipped her glass over. This excited more laughter and attention from the others in the bar. But these women did not care what the bar rabble were thinking. They were so overwhelmed by this sudden risibility they could not have contained themselves had they desired to. And they laughed as women will do at times in the powder room of a gala event, or in the kitchen of a house without men.

When their hilarity did finally subside and the women regained their composure, Mary said to her friend, "Mr. Fred speaks like the Good Book but he must not hear his own words."

"Yes," said Selma, "He has a wife but he covets his working girls. Mr. Fred has no soul. But he is a good man. He has pleased both of us."

"He is fine," agreed Mary. "I do not despise him."

The women paid their bill and left the bar. They went back to the flat and went straight to bed without washing their faces. They slumbered heavily that night with the alcohol in them. Each one dreamt of the other.

The next morning, Selma woke up with the suspicion that she had been given a gift. She believed she felt the weight of it at the foot of the bed. But she could not yet lift her pained head up to see. What had she dreamed about exactly? She wondered. Was it of the gesture of a hand, a lovely hand reaching out to her? And did she put out her own hand to meet it? Yes she did! She remembered then, the amber warmth and swell of that touch. She had held the gift in her hand; this gift that was not hers alone but the other's also. The giver was the gift. Selma put her small, iron-burnt hand into the hand and knew that this was not the hand of the Man from Galilee, the one of which so much has been said. She had not felt a fraternal hold. No, what she felt was something more compelling and graceful. Maybe it was the outstretched hand of a laughing black Madonna. She couldn't tell. All she knew was that she felt there, in the palm, the flooding warmth of a love the color and intensity of precious gemstones.

Still lying in bed, Selma tried to stretch her legs out but there was a lump at the end of the bed that precluded her from fully extending. She lifted herself up to see what was there. It was Mary in fact, who was sleeping horizontally at the foot of the bed. She did not wake Mary up but quietly got herself out of bed and dressed. Mary however, would have appreciated being woke up for she was having an odious dream. She was dreaming that Selma, propped up on the bed like a Queen, was reading off a list of men's names, names of lovers past and to come, and that with the reading of each name she herself grew more and more ill with nausea and vertigo. When Mary finally did get up, she discovered she had a hangover.

That following year was perhaps the happiest Selma had ever known. She had a lover and a friend to share him with and she could not have asked for more. Mary, who had always skirted away from Selma's attempts to thicken their friendship with secrets and privy revelations, became without intending to do so in the least, her intimate friend, her sisterly confidant. What could be more intimate after all, than sharing a lover? Their hearts and loins craved similarly. It was as if one could not love Mr. Fred without the help of the other. As for Mr. Fred, he was really quite a man, visiting as regularly as always, leaving each woman satisfied when he left. He lost a little weight but this suited him well and did not signal poor health. A generous man in his own way, he bought the roommates a floor heater as in winter it did get terribly cold in the flat. None of them thought this arrangement an odd one. This was simply the way they lived and it was a very small part of their living indeed for most of the time they worked. All three of them worked very hard to get ahead and only Mr. Fred got ahead. But this too, none of them found strange. Every day the girls worked from eight till six with an one hour lunch break to eat a sandwich. In the evening they liked to drink a coco-punch before dinner while taking birdbaths in the sink. After dinner they would wait for Mr. Fred who always came with a bottle tucked under his arm. He wore exceedingly large brown belts with silver buckles. He thought that the ladies appreciated this. Saturday afternoons and Sundays the girls had off and these days they spent together, going to the picture show or window shopping. Selma would ask Mary, "Do you want to see to all those shop windows today?" And Mary would say, "Yes please." Selma always made the suggestions and Mary was ever agreeing to them. In this way, they were inseparable.

What Selma did not care to realize was that this well-being and security she so needed and had then, was dependent upon Mary's disposition to yield. Mary had always complied with Selma's desires and wants. There was a "Yes please" or a "Yes, I will" waiting at the tip of her tongue for any occasion to agree. But what if Mary were not to submit, what if she were not to act in accordance? Selma did not want to think of this. She dismissed such thoughts immediately when they came to mind. She believed she knew her friend, as well as herself even. Yes, looking at Mary was like looking in the mirror. She knew what she would see and what comfort in knowing! Their wants were mutual wants. Why they drank from the same cup! The cup of the disciples. But whom were they following? Selma would have to admit it was herself. This was her bliss.

It was true that Mary was of a compliant nature, however, as natures do change so did hers, rather dramatically even, as far as the suddenness of it, although without any theatrics, for Mary was a humble girl. Her change was first expressed by a polite refusal. Selma asked her one Sunday morning if she wanted to go to the movies and Mary said in her usual lilting voice, "No thank you," without qualms and without explanation. Selma was stunned dumb. She went in the kitchen to brush her teeth and nothing more was said. Mary left the apartment before she. This was the first day they had spent apart in over a year. Selma was very weepy and cried throughout the movie she went to see although it wasn't a sad movie in the least. In fact it was a burlesque comedy. When the women had dinner that night nothing was said about Mary's diversion. Indeed things seemed to be quite normal and the week went by as usual, with exhausting work at the sweatshop, coco-punch, and Mr. Fred's visits. But the following Sunday, Mary again said, "No thank you," and left on her own to seek for herself what she was wanting. This put Selma in a terrible emotional quandary. She wanted to ask of her friend, "But where are you going without me? Why do you not say 'Yes please' as before?" But she was put to silence by her own heart which could not have supported the answer, which could not bear even the question. She was forlorn and tried to gain her friend's affection back with small gifts, gold lamé barrettes for the hair and iced cakes from a noted patisserie. But she saw with dismay that this was too facile for although Mary was delighted with these gifts she continued to abandon her, oblivious it seemed, to the sorrow this brought her.

It then came to be that Mary would leave work at six and not come home for the night. How this tormented Selma! Mr. Fred came but there was no longer any joy in it. She could hardly be a woman to him. And she grew impatient of his antics which before she had found titillating. She began to loathe him and to see herself as the most loathsome of women. "Stop that, Mr. Fred!" she would yell at him irritably. "Can't you see that's not how it's done?" The poor man was at loss and began to miss the other woman who was always so accommodating and quiet. Selma missed her too, terribly so and some evenings she would cry and ask to be comforted. Mr. Fred comforted her a bit then he stopped coming at all. Selma was alone. She knew Mary had taken a lover, and she understood that this one was not to be shared. And while this secrecy hurt her she did not care so much about it, she wanted more than anything else for Mary to come home. "Please, dear Mary come home, come home!" she would whimper to herself before falling asleep.

Mary did finally come home, bringing with her the man with whom she had disappeared. She introduced him as Mr. Jones and he was the tallest, whitest and most elegantly dressed man either girl had ever seen. His skin and hair were so perfectly white that when one looked at him they produced a glare. He wore dark glasses too and only Mary knew that this was because he had very sensitive, pink eyes that could not take the light. He was, of course, an albino but neither girl could have named the magnificent alabaster strangeness of him. Mr. Jones was an Englishman.

"I am here to take my suitcase and cosmetics trunk. I am going with Mr. Jones to London. He says it is a very nice town."

Selma, who was fighting back her tears, searched desperately for words to keep her friend from going.

"You are leaving with this Mr. Snowman? Now, you are really a crazy girl. What do you know about such snowmen? I've heard that they will eat you! Yes! They will eat women and give the bones to their dogs. I have read this, believe me! You must not go with him! You must stay here with me and Mr. Fred. Don't you want to stay with us?"

To this Mary said, "No thank you." And she took her bags. And she left the one-room flat for good to go to the city of London.

Anyone who is living a full life knows then, what it is to live through devastation. This is what Selma suffered for two months. It would be perhaps tiresome to detail the angst and despair of such a time. Selma herself wondered how long she could bear her own lachrymose state. But it took her two months to grieve her loss and when her mourning was over, she decided to leave Paris and sweat shop number twenty-seven and the rue Casimir du Loup, to go back to Turkey where her family was eagerly awaiting her. She packed her bags and made her way to the eighty-six-hour bus to Istanbul.

On this bus she happened to sit next to an elderly woman draped with reddish-hued shawls. She was most

42

affable and spoke with Selma about her life in Paris. She was a fortune teller and had had a long-standing practice in Paris and in Nice and was heading back to Turkey to retire. When the eighty-six-hour bus made a brief pit stop, the women went into the roadside cafeteria where they had stopped for some refreshment. Selma ordered an apple tart with coffee and it was the grounds of this cup of coffee that the fortune-teller read.

"I see," she said, "that you will only be at your family's breast for a short while. You will make a trip to the northern countries where it is very green and cold. You will find yourself very happy in one of these countries and decide to stay there. And here, yes, I see it, you will meet a very pale man whose skin lacks color but whose heart is warm. You will stay by his side."

Selma thanked her for this and felt her toes, fingers, and breasts tingle for the first time in so long, with the glimmer of hope. Her thoughts gathered less around the hope of having a man for the sake of a singular and conjugal event, than around the prospect of meeting a partible man, one that can and must be divided and shared, the heritable property of a beloved friend. She sought that man who could be endured jointly. To be alone with a man, she felt, was to be very alone indeed. She could no longer fathom the desire for it. She thought of Mr. Fred; he had come, stayed, and then he had left. He left when there was no longer anything to share, no longer any gift. There was nothing to pass from one loving hand to the next. The gift! Where had it gone?

The eighty-six-hour bus continued on in the night. "Ah," said Selma quietly to herself, "My Friend."

The Lost and Found

Dulce María O'Riley de Vaca lived in a one-room flat above a Moroccan disco on the rue des Quatres Camemberts. She dined alone; she prepared haricots alone; she made love alone on occasion. Was she lonely? No, but she was alone. At least a good part of the day. She did have some time on her hands and was learning to claim it, although not as her own exactly. She might demand her due and then sift the deed through her fingertips mischievously. That was how much she cared to own a moment. Oh not a bit! On her birthday, the concierge gave her a pressure cooker for quicker minute rice but she used it to keep her lingerie in instead. No, she was not an avid timekeeper. Sometimes she wistfully said, "Time is passing and I no longer hear the clocks." So you see, Dulce María was somewhat deaf. Once she procured a Gideons' Bible from a hotel in Zimbabwe. She had been invited there by a geologist who had promised her an emerald tiara for her visit. Only he never showed up and she spent two weeks in a bungalo at the Hippo Lounge Lodge where she developed an intimate liaison with a member of the help. She helped herself.

Dulce María held down a part-time job as a claqueur in the afternoons. That is to say she was a hired applauder for a television game show called "Objets Trouvés," or rather "The Lost and Found." For four years she had been clapping for the "Lost and Found Show." And she knew a variety of plaudits: the clap of bereavement for the loser, the pom-pom clap for the nearly lost, the encore clap for the blessed, and the Lancaster clap. She was a specialist of the last which was simply a marimba clap that she would do for a somebody she might care to see again. Yes, she did sometimes break the rules set by game-show host Pierre Lescault and make appointment dates with the guest star players. Pierre Lescault was worried about losing his ill-paid and uninsured claqueurs to the nouveaux riches and forbade their lingering in the coulisse. Mostly though, he was ignored and considered a burr. In fact it was back-stage after a show that Dulce María met the Zimbabwean geologist. He had been the grand-prize winner. He received the Lancaster clap and a congratulatory invitation to the corner café. He went. They had a hot thing for a while. Then he didn't show up at the Hippo Lounge Lodge and she reckoned herself a fool. Hadn't her mother warned her time and again? Yes, she could still hear her mother's voice, a voice of lulling and unsympathetic wisdom. She remembered the conversation they had had during her last visit home in Mexico.

"Dulce María, you must never trust a man of promises. Your breasts are too large. Remember this."

"My breasts are nothing," she said back. "Your breasts are bigger than mine and your husband comes home to them every night. Breasts are not confusing. They are there or they're not."

"You are right, my husband does come home every night. But he is not a man of promises. He has promised me nothing and I have nothing. I have never expected more from him. Now your father, that was a man of promises. And where is he today? I was young when I met him and he promised me a villa on the Calle de los Novios, a chandelier in the boudoir, and a bidet. I believed him and was hopeful. Then I became pregnant with you while still in the home of my parents. I received in the mail one day a postcard from Austria. It was from your father. 'Where is Austria?' I asked myself. 'It is far away,' I answered. There have been four other postcards, all of them sent from distant countries. That is your father, Dulce María, a man of promises."

"But mother, if a man makes no promises there is little hope for things to come. And hardly any pleasure in the waiting."

"Yes, this is true and it is better this way. You will learn to love the lesser surprises, the extra egg in the hatch, a kind word from a lecherous man, the end of a curse. Dulce María, if a man promises you something and if it is a house, tell him to take you there straight away with the keys so that you can walk in and urinate in the foyer. If this maddens the man, then you know that he has been insincere with you. If he takes this calmly and inquires

49

after your health, then you may rest assured that he will do good by you."

Dulce María shook her head in acknowledgment of this advice but quit her mother feeling dissatisfied and bewildered. No man had ever promised her a house before. She wouldn't know what this meant were it to happen. As for piddling in the hallway of a strange home, this seemed much too complicated and nasty to Dulce María. She wished she were as courageous as her mother, as straightforward and accepting. She saw her so rarely since she had left home but often thought of her briskly going about her daily errands with a straw push cart. She knew that trajectory by heart. The mother of Dulce María went to the outdoor market at the Plaza Espoza every morning and was meticulous about the meats she bought.

"Where is this chicken from?" she asked the poulterer.

"From the farm of my brother, Victor." he would answer.

"Of course, but when was its neck rung?"

"This morning at half past six."

"Then where are its feet and feathers?"

"In the bucket."

"Then you must fetch the bucket."

"But it is not here."

"Then go and find it. I will buy the chicken when you can show me."

The poulterer would go back to his truck to look for the bucket of plucked chicken remains. For his own pride and for the pride of his brother he did this. And when he came back waving a bucket of poultry crud he shouted, "Behold!" The mother of Dulce María would look into the bucket, point vaguely to a foot, nod her head and purchase the chicken. She was so thoroughly cool, so painfully exacting. And she spared no merchant her standards of perfection, not even the decrepit Señora del Cruz, whose corn was sometimes spotted with a smut disease, although she sat with them all at mass and took their hands almost lovingly for the kiss of peace. She did not trust them. Dulce María on the other hand, lacked market savvy entirely. Indeed, she had the poorest of market skills and was more often than not left overcharged and undernourished after the open-air marché on the rue des Quatre Camemberts. Her mother's pleasurable rigor was her guilt. And her daily penance came as imprudent purchases, a bag of verminous walnuts, a bottle of soured milk, five insipid grapefruits from Israel. Yes, in the market she was a doltish girl. Usually she took her meal at the "Objets Trouvés" cafeteria before clapping.

When Dulce María decided to leave her family in Mexico to go to Paris, she hoped in a vague way that she might come across her father, Jude O'Riley there. It was just a fantasy of sorts, a long shot at that, and she only remotely acknowledged it. Perhaps this was prudent of her. In any case, she eventually forgot she had even harbored the notion. Her father was an Irishman. She knew very little about him except that he had committed a demeaning crime in Ireland and so sought asylum from a pecuniary penalty in Mexico where he met the lovely peasant girl Juanita Vaca de Luz, her mother. He promised her many things, impregnated her, and then left the continent. Dulce María suspected she resembled her father, for she looked nothing like her mother. She was a fair complected, strawberry blond and exceeded her mother, a diminutive, swarthy woman, in height by seven inches. As an adolescent she had been nicknamed La Rojona. She was quite an anomaly. She wept bitterly often and yelled when nobody could hear, "I am not the Big Red One. I am not the Big Red One." That she blossomed into the swan at the age of twenty was an act of faith. The faith of her mother. She never despaired but kept a stronghold of beliefs, and prayed for pulchritude and feminine grace and womanly attributes, that all this be bestowed on her daughter. Dulce María had become a beauty indeed.

Yes, Dulce María was quite beautiful but she was also difficult. For this reason she lived alone. When she had lovers, they came and went but did not settle in. Few people readily took to her. She stuttered a bit and was verbally awkward. She was a polyglot though and sometimes heard symphonies in her left ear. In the morning Dulce María would get up rather early and fix herself a continental breakfast while still in her shimmy. Her mornings were languorous, vulnerable to delicacies and disasters, and she structured them gently by reading the papers. She read at least four of them, swiftly looking over the front pages and distressing headline stories, then lingering over the personals. They could fill her with such hope. There might be a set of Italian clutch bags to be sold immediately at discount advertised, or a wealthy American industrialist seeking girl Friday live-in at penthouse. Several times she had seen the ad: "Earn one thousand francs a day without leaving your home." She even called for more information but the line was busy. Yes, if anything really did go wrong, she knew she could seek help in the personals. There were a myriad of possibilities. How comforting it was for her to know this.

It was while going through the personals one morning that she stumbled upon the following ad, "Thank you sacred heart of Jesus and Saint Jude for prayers answered." She found this curious although she couldn't have said why. She tried to remember the import of St. Jude in the hagiology but couldn't rightly place him. He was in any case her father's patron saint. Dulce María felt there was something secular and crass about thanking the sacred hearts of Saint Jude and Jesus in this way. Still, she did wonder at it. The following day she came across the same ad although not only in the paper she had seen it in last time but in two others also. The day after that, the same. Then she had a dream. In this dream she was walking along the Río Doloroso of her homeland. It was a torpid afternoon and there were angels flying in the white sky. One of them, a flaming redhead, flying directly above her and playing the violin, shat on her shoulder. She was reviled and yelled, "May the sacred heart of Saint Jude clip your wings and make spittle on your fiddle!" And upon the utterance of these words, the angel fell impotently to the ground and his violin melted into a salivary puddle. Dulce María awoke from this dream feeling anxious. Rather than have her continental breakfast right away as she usually did, she threw a coat on over her chemise, slipped into sneakers, and went out to the kiosk where she bought four papers. She went back upstairs, made some coffee, and sat down to read. She flipped directly to the personals and ran her finger down the columns, scanning the announcements exigently. Her hand stopped at the following one:

May the Sacred Heart of Jesus be adored, glorified, and perpetuated forever. Sacred Heart of Jesus pray for us. Saint Jude hope for the hopeless, pray for us. Saint Jude, worker of miracles, pray for us. (Repeat nine times for nine days. Publication must be promised.) J.O.

She circled it with a pink high lighter. Then she went on to do a crossword puzzle to quiet her nerves. But she was too agitated to focus on that and so went down to the market to get some fruit. She bought some mangoes, effortlessly for once, and milled about while trying to decide what else to get. She passed by a stand selling blood oranges. They looked good to her and she queued up. There were two people before her in line, an old stumpy woman and a man, a very smart-looking carrot top. He was being helped at that moment and turned toward Dulce María to indicate the kiwis. He took no notice of her, however; he was intent on the fruit. But she did see him; she couldn't, in fact, keep her eyes off him. "I know that man," she was saying to herself, "Yes, I have seen him before. He's so familiar." She tried to remember where she might have crossed paths with him but her thoughts were interrupted by the fruit vendor who asked her what she wanted. She asked for oranges and was shortchanged. When she turned around to look for the man, he was nowhere to be seen. She wandered through the marketplace for a while looking, then gave up and headed back to her apartment.

Dulce María got ready for work. She took a shower

and powdered herself. She polished her shoes and pinned her hair in a chignon. Then she brushed her teeth. It was as she was doing this that she made the connection she had been trying to make all morning since she had seen the man in the market. "He's the fallen angel. Yes, that's he! The one I had sacked by the Sacred Heart of St. Jude." She was marveled and excited. Then fearful. She had, after all, provoked his shameful descent by her invocation. Why had she done that? But it was just a dream she told herself. She could hardly be held responsible. As for the man in the market, he was real, she hadn't dreamed him. He was buying kiwis. She left for the "Objets Trouvés" studio and clapped the whole afternoon. Bless her heart. She really did clap a lot. That night she soaked her hands in buttermilk and went to bed exhausted.

The following morning she got up sluggishly and bumped her head on a cupboard while making breakfast. Again, she read the papers and again she found the prayer to St. Jude, the very same one. She read it nine times. She was struck by one line particularly. It was, "Saint Jude hope for the hopeless, pray for us," and she repeated it aloud. Ah! She heard herself then! She was one of the hopeless. A hopeless, marginal girl who applauded on cue and accepted invitations from unemployed men. Now, many would think it strange that a beautiful woman could have considered herself in this way, but Dulce María, it has been mentioned, was also difficult. She did not know how to get by on her good looks as is said. She was much too taken with her own difficulty to be this clever. She had never learned. And so she felt very hopeless indeed. She saw herself as pitiful and unpromising. She had even struck down what was perhaps her guardian angel because he had done something unappealing. Oh, she had no charity either! Yet there was the thought of someone that lightened Dulce María's anguish. It was St. Jude. Yes. He was the Hope of the Hopeless. He was the worker of miracles. "Blessed Heart of Saint Jude," she prayed, "prove to me that I am the daughter of both man and woman and I will adore, glorify, and perpetuate you." Then she knew what she was to do. For nine days she would repeat the invocation nine times and on the ninth day run the prayer in the personals. She began to feel a renewal of faith. Yes, she would be alright. Saint Jude's sacred heart would attend to her. His prayer was his promise, and if the former were followed meticulously, the latter would be fulfilled.

The first day of the nine days of invocation went like this: Dulce María said the prayer just before going to work. She said it in deep concentration with her eyes closed. When she got to the studio she took her seat and waited for the show to start. Three red-wigged clowns appeared as contestants on the stage that day. The joker's wild! Good God!

On the second day she was offered a ride by a real estate promoter named James. He drove an orange Peugot. She refused.

The third day she bought red hot pants and wore them under a pleated skirt.

The evening of the fourth day she was lured into the Moroccan disco below her apartment and served a Bloody Mary cocktail.

The fifth day she painted her toenails Chinese red and ate a hot pepper.

On the sixth day she menstruated.

The seventh day she accidentally bought a pomegranate and stained her shirt.

On the eighth day she was offered a stick of cherry-flavored gum.

The ninth day she sat down and wrote the prayer on a piece of stationary. She wrote:

Sacred heart of Saint Jude pray for us. Saint Jude hope for the hopeless, pray for us. Saint Jude, worker of miracles, pray for us. May you be adored and perpetuated. May the father of Dulce María O'Riley de Vaca find his daughter. May he indicate his whereabouts in the personals. Loving hearts of Jesus and Saint Jude pray for us now and at the hour of our deaths. D.M.O. de V.

Dulce María folded the letter and put it in an envelope. She wrote a check for fifty francs and put that in too. Then she went to the post office to mail it. She was feeling intrepid as she walked down the rue des Quatre Camemberts, so invulnerable, so protected by that divine office. Why, she could have walked in front of a passing car and not have been hit. She was sure of it. She could have asked for a pearl and been given it. Everything free of charge for Dulce María, everything in the palm of her hand! It was all so simple. Why hadn't she thought of it before? Hadn't she always been told, Ask and you shall receive? And now St. Jude was on her side. That had to be a plus. Upon her supplication he had chastised the angel who offended her.

Just for the asking! "I am learning something," Dulce María said to herself with a quiet sense of self-satisfaction. "It has been so long that I haven't learned anything but now I am learning."

On the tenth day her ad appeared and she read it with great pleasure. She cut it out and hung it on her wall. Then she went out and bought herself a pastry. She sat down at the terrace of a café with the soft March sun on her and bathed in the warmth and kindness of it. She was radiant. Her skin glistened and her luminous green eyes looked upon the street scene brazenly. Everything was delightful presage: a young girl found a bracelet in the gutter; a pigeon found its mate; the waiter found a five-franc tip in an ashtray. It was a morning of hallowed portent. Many men passed and eyed her appealingly. Dulce María had lovely breasts.

When she scanned through the personals on the eleventh day, she did not find what she had hoped to. She sighed and knocked on the wooden cross above her bed. She told herself to be patient and then felt virtuous. On the twelveth day there was still nothing and she thought of Calvary and of the stigmata. She received an unexpected call from the Zimbabwean geologist. She met him that evening and they made love in a tugboat, docked along the Canal de l'Ourcq. This consoled her for a time.

Then an entire week passed without any response, and Dulce María was burdened, burdened by her own cross. The cross of hope. Hope was her obligation. What had once made her giddy and alert, now dulled her like an addiction. It was not a question of loss of hope. She couldn't have lost it without its being taken away from her. It was like that. She bore her cross.

But then twelve days after the appearance of her ad in the paper, there was finally a response. Dulce María read it like one who reads her destiny, that is to say, trembling, with the eyes nearly shut. It read:

May the Sacred Heart of Jesus be adored, glorified, and perpetuated forever. Saint Jude hope for the hopeless, pray for us. Saint Jude, worker of miracles, pray for us. May the father of Sweet Mary O'Riley meet his daughter on the steps of the Opera today at four. May she remind him of her mother. Sacred Heart of Jesus and Saint Jude pray for us sinners now and always.

Dulce María's mind raced as she digested the message. First of all she would have to call in sick to work. As for looking like her mother, this distressed her as she didn't resemble the woman in the least. She decided to wear a poncho and carry a woven basket. That would have to do. Then she dropped to her knees and said the invocation nine times. Her cheeks were flushed and she cried out, "My God, My God, you have not forsaken me. How good of you!" Her body rocked with emotion. "Saint Jude, may the bounty of your sacred heart be known to all! I have known it!"

At a quarter of four, Dulce María was sitting on the steps leading up to the Opera. She had on her turquoise poncho. There were others there too. A group of Japanese girls with drawing pads sat to her right. An African man was selling watches and other wares from a black suitcase. Fatigued tourists, demonstrative couples, and the lovelorn sat on the steps along with Dulce María. She did not feel conspicuous, even though her poncho was florid. She was surprisingly calm, calm enough to read a book. That is until four o'clock. At four she shut her book and began watching. She watched actively, so attentively in truth that she didn't notice the time pass by. When she did look at her watch, it was four thirty. A pang of anxiety made her stand up for a moment. "Blessed Saint Jude!" Then a cacophony of sirens heralded out from all sides of the opera and police trucks, cars, and motorcycles raced by but were soon caught up in traffic and had to maneuver their way adroitly through the maze of cars. It was pandemonium. The sirens did not fade out in the distance but lingered and insisted at the spot. Cars honked and there were several superfluous bumper accidents. The Japanese girls watched all this and clapped. Dulce María clapped with them for a moment, automatically and without joy. Eventually the cavalcade passed through and headed, it seemed, toward the Place Vendôme. Dulce María who had been standing up throughout the scene, sat back down on the step and looked at her watch. It was ten after five. "This isn't good but perhaps he has been stuck in the traffic. I will wait a half hour more." And so she waited, eyes riveted on the passers-by. Had she been a smoker, she would not have smoked. This was how thoroughly she waited. And although she was losing faith by the minute, and cursing St. Jude between her teeth, she waited still. There was no pleasure in this expectancy. It was her cross and weighed heavy on her back. She could not get up from beneath it. She tarried and abstained from idle conversa-

tion with the Japanese. She was being sketched, gro-
tesquely by some, but paid no attention.

At six o'clock several policemen came along, asking the
public to clear the steps for there was to be an official
soirée in honor of the ministers of state. Dulce María was
helped to her feet by a bearded gendarme. She was limp
and feeble and the bearded man had to steady her for a
moment. She said in her language, "Saint Jude, Saint Jude,
why have you forsaken me? I ought to be the daughter of
man and woman but shall never know this." She was
escorted to a taxi line and put into a blue cab by firm
hands. On the ride home her mind was filled with visions
of the procession of saints. There was St. Miguel, St. Joaquin, St. Jorge El Guapo, and St. Francisco El Hulmilde.
And so many more. They passed by her in a virile parade,
chests puffed out and so on, and as each pious face turned
toward her, it contorted horribly in mocking laughter.

When the taxi reached the rue des Quatre Camemberts,
Dulce María got out and breathed in the brisk evening air.
There were no more saints in her head, the procession
perhaps continued elsewhere but it was then outside her
vision. She regained her vigor and walked briskly up the
stairs to her apartment. When she was inside, she took the
personals she had saved and put them in a brown paper
bag. She gathered all her prayer cards from the top dresser
drawer and her wallet and put them in too. Then she lit
the bag with a match and threw it, burning, out the window. She lived on the fourth floor. "May the Sacred Heart
of Saint Jude . . ." she started. Then she laughed, as wickedly as the saints themselves. She laughed at herself and at

the duplicity of the angels. This devilishness made her terribly hungry and she got herself some blood oranges. She ate them ravenously. She even ate the skins. Sitting with her legs stretched out in front of her and leaning on a pouffe, her mother's voice came back to her. Never trust a man of promises, she had said many times. Dulce María thought to herself, "A man of promises and a saint of hope. One and the same."

The next day Dulce María did not buy the newspapers as usual. She no longer saw the need for that. Instead she bought a financial magazine of sorts. She decided that she would go to the university. She wanted to be an economist. This was how she began to claim her own fate and time.

If she had, however, read the paper that day and if she had looked on page A6, she would have seen the picture of Jude O'Riley, the man in the market, the fallen angel, her father. He had been arrested for holding up a very famous *bijouterie* next door to the Ritz at the Place Vendôme. In the photo he had on a very nice suit with a bow tie. Yes, he looked most congenial. He held a black wig in his hand. His own hair was disheveled and standing straight up on end. The headline read, "International Jewelry Thief 'Carrot Top' O'Riley Found in Ritz Hotel Barbershop."

A prayer to Saint Jude could not have done better. With the paper between her hands she would have seen and believed. For whatever that might have been worth. But Dulce María did not bother with the papers. And it should be said that she was rarely disappointed from then on. She didn't need a patron of lost causes. She wasn't hopeless. She was merely betrayed. Ah Judas!

Like Father Like Son

I am the son of the Professor Touré, seer and African medium. Many people come to my father, the Professor Touré, with trouble and difficulties. Many black people, many white people. Many women. Many women desiring fertility. More women looking for the Good Boy. The Professor Touré accepts credit cards, checks, and travelers checks with identification and the clientele is grateful to him for this. They say to him, "For you I will no longer do this wrong thing. I will quit it. I will give it up." And mens come to the Professor Touré who knows well what's in the hearts of mens, and say, "I'm really not a chain-drinker anymore." My father musts see if they truly reject the drink and gives them a beer. If he finds they don't reject, he will say, "You do drink the beer a bit, yes?" And the mens see that what they are doing is bad and very soon later stop being silly. Sure. A woman will come to my father and ask, "When will I meet the Golden Boy?" The Professor Touré tells her, "You must patient yourself, he is around your corner but is not hurried. His pockets are weighted down with coins. When he comes you will lighten his load and breathe the fresher air." Most pay my father with cash notes but he is regularized with the French government and accepts all those plastic cards and checks.

On Wednesdays from six until eleven, the Professor Touré does the minitel consultation. The clients tap 36 15 Touré on the Minitel and reach him this way. I appreciate the minitel because if one can have a phone, one can have this too, without costing except for the use. And as a result all has one and many call my father. I know the Minitel well because I'm a student of Computer or Informatic Sciences. For this reason I am presently in France living with my father who is doing solid work and so is paying my inscriptions. Before I was living in Nigeria with my mother, the third wife of the Professor Touré. Now I discover my father. In a year I will enter the University of Mathematics and Informatic Science. But at this time I'm much at learning this French language at the school and at the house. I study there much, too. Although there are many consultations and all the time my father, the Professor Touré, is working to disenchant those in spellbound or to find the loved one again. This can make terrible noises and racquets so that my head doesn't stay in the model books very well. But I will have results because it musts be so. Because my father has seen my vision and it just be a good one of me with many computers and a happier account book at the Commercial Bank. Sure.

I have always done my bests and as a result badness doesn't circulate in my body. Mens and women come to my father with this evil in their bellies and limbs and the Professor Touré lifts it out in the two days ahead of them. He gives them a list of right foods, all those beginning with the letter "Q" and tells them to heed with strictest concern. No Betrayal! And those people have better blood again.

Because my father lives as the bachelor, I help him when cooking and ironing. His wives live in five countries of Africa. He is now the continental man who doesn't marry but has sweeties. There's Sweetie I and Sweetie II, Sweetie III and Sweetie IV, Sweetie V and Sweetie VI. Then there are the not-so-sweet who come too, and do washing up and his bidding. None of the sweeties has keys to this life-flat but all arrive inside alright, with no key. These sweeties are clever making my father sometimes lose his faculty a bit.

In Nigeria, like my father, I had the sweeties also. In this way, I was as the Professor Touré. But I don't look like he. It is said I look American. I am so tall that my head, it touching the lid of the metro train. And all that hair cutting; it done by Monsieur Bobo who was going to New York very much and to Miami and to Los Angeles. He knows how those mens live and hair cut. When I came to Paris I was sixteen and a half. Today I am seventeen and have a Paris girlfriend, never forgetting the opportunity of others and more. She is called Sylvie-Anne Dubaix. She's the prettier one I saw sitting at the Palais Royal. My French is poor but I'm learning it at the language school and at home and at the home of Sylvie-Anne. When I first met Sylvie-Anne, I musts tell her, "You don't know me from the other mens. Maybe you think I'm a bad man. But I'm not the bad man. I am from a good family in the city of Lagos. My uncle is a dentist." And this good day I succeeded to have Sylvie-Anne's telephone number which I called on Monday and on Tuesday and on Wednesday and on Thursday. Friday she met me at the Café Pompadour and I buy her the tiny coffee she asks and tell her what's on my mind. First I tell her: "Sylvie-Anne, when you are with a Nigerian man, you are not with a Frenchman. And as a result, the romance isn't the same one as the Frenchmen. Roses and hand kissing, not these things. But the Blackman, he is strong. Yes, Blackmens are strong ones. And when a white woman makes love to the Blackman, she will no longer be enjoying the whiteman. After she doesn't take pleasure with the whiteman. Sure. I tell you this and it is true."

Sylvie-Anne believes me and as a result, I come and go and visit the house of Sylvie-Anne often and often. She gives me a door key and I keepsake it. There are many lovelier girls in Paris city but Sylvie-Anne has long red hair like the lightning flower. And this makes her a beautiful one. She has so nice hands and uses them with me and my hands too, need to use themselves with her. As a result we are ever touching.

But a week ago, there was a happening that troubled me. My father, the Professor Touré, was in consultation and I, right next to his official door, learning at the desk, heard the goings-on a bit. I was hearing a bit and learning a bit. Then I was hearing that voice that I know. I said to myself, "the voice of Sylvie-Anne is there in the consultation room." Here, I put my ear on the door and hear very well indeed that voice of my Paris girlfriend. So I was thinking.

"Professor Touré," she asks, "When will I meet my Golden Boy. At the moment I amuse myself with a young man but this is insufficient." Here I want to open the door and defend my honorable, but my father speaks and I remember him and all respect for his wisdom.

"Your Golden Boy," he says, "will be wearing a green and gold cap as an American. But he will not be American. You will meet him in a tobacco shop as he's buying a stamp book."

"Will he speak to me, or need I address him first?" she asks.

"Ah," says the Professor Touré, "That I do not tell you. In any case you know that you are spoken to and speak."

I could hear her taking out all those bills to pay. And I think of her little hands and painty nails that's so pretty and doing it all. But then I was knowing how to be her Golden Boy for truth. It's being a matter of a cap and a stamp. My father might not know he arranged me but he did so. Sure.

The next morning, and here I was leaving early so to be the first one, I went to the hat shop and got the green and gold one that would make me more American enough and then I go to Sylvie-Anne's and wait, ever hiding in my trench coat beside a tree. Sylvie-Anne does not go out of her house before eleven o'clock. But she comes out then and looking more the lightning flower than before. Her reddy hair so long that it touching her bottom. She walks the street with a shopping bag and goes to the Chinese grocery, I following some footsteps behind of her. I don't go into Chinese grocery but wait outside. She comes out with a bag of fruits and some fishes and walks more til she arrives secondly at the dry cleaners. Here she waits in the line and the cleaner man, he smiling at her, very charmer as Frenchmens do. She waits after her affairs and he goes to gets them and when he comes again there are no more clients except Sylvie-Anne. This cleaner man has a mustache like the water buffalo horns and thinks he is pleasing her with it. Maybe so. But Sylvie-Anne, she doesn't stay long, just long so as to gets her affairs. And so she pays the cleaner man and walks out. And her hair, it jumps against her bottom so pretty and as a result the cleaner man is looking at her and longing.

Then I see that on the corner is the tobacco shop to where Sylvie-Anne goes to gets her cigarettes. She smokes the filtered ones which are the better ones for ladies, I think. It behooves her to gets these kinds.

It was necessary to gets there before she, so that I was wearing the cap and buying the stamps as she was coming in. I was very speedy indeed and rushed there to first put on my cap and looking American enough, to go to that counter.

So Sylvie-Anne enters and I, who am standing near the counter but not on it, go on it and order the stamp book. Sylvie-Anne, she is behind me a bit and musts only see the cap and my hand on the stamps. Then I turn around and say, "Hello, Sylvie-Anne," lifting my cap and waving high the stamp collection. "It is very good to see you in such a surprising morning time." And so she says hello to me and kisses me as the usual way. I am not understanding that she looks at me and doesn't know she looks at her Golden Boy. As a result I ask her, "Do you look at my hat?"

"That's a nice cap," she says and nothing more adding. She is not shocking in the least. Then I ask her if she be needing some stamps for all those epistles Paris girls write and she replies me, "No, I don't write." Sylvie-Anne orders her filtered cigarettes and asks me to help her carry her bags of affairs to her house.

"But Sylvie-Anne," I ask her, "Am I not your Golden Boy?"

"No," says she, "I don't believe you are. And why should you be? This hardly matters."

She, all the while throwing her long, reddy hair about as a Parisian girl in truth. And so I become desperation and know I musts tell what I am knowing as she is misunderstanding.

"You are told by the Professor Touré that your Golden Boy musts meet you wearing a green and gold cap and buying stamp books. Look! He is me! Look at me, look at me! I am here!"

And she is looking at me like I am crazy man and says, "Whatever are you talking about?" and leaves speedy to carry her bags alone.

My father, the Professor Touré, is never wrong and musts guarantee results. But I am his new son in Paris and do not always hear that French voice well and am confusing one for another. And the Parisian woman's voice is mostly the same one, like the birds all at once in the baobab tree. And so as I write this, I haven't that French sweetie I had. I am farewell to her. But I am in this Paris city and there are many nest to know still. Many and more sweeties often and pleasing. Sure.

• • •

There were five messages left on my answering machine today. All were from the same man, each one more insistant than the one before. They were the same: "Nurse Lime-Away, I musts speaks to you. You musts pick up this phone so that I can speak to you. You musts take this phone. You know what I am meaning."

It has been a trying day at the Hôtel Dieu. At four o'clock the firemen of the nineteenth arrondissement arrived and were bedded in the burn ward although most of them weren't burned badly but rather asphyxiated and fatigued from great municipal efforts. This is to say there were fifteen *pompiers* to undress then dress in no-hook hospital smocks. And they were left as all Patients of Life, bare legged and barer bottomed. By the end of the day I was exhausted and when I arrived home and listened to the messages, I was clearly distraught. I went back out the door and to the florist where I bought two potted geraniums. This was my gesture of self-forgiveness. For I have once again betrayed, although perhaps aptly enough to be considered fashionable, which is why I can take the confession in my own hands. And weigh my potted sins, one in the left and another in the right. I'll listen to them flourish and tick and become something else entirely. My dear absolution.

As for my betrayal, I've mercly betrayed in the commonest of ways, which, it seems to me, is far worse than deceiving oneself unusually. At least an exceptionally grave betrayal can lead one to the Extraordinary or to the glimmer of a precipice much desired. But my betrayal involves a young man. So you see, it is very commonplace indeed.

The young man's name is Wilfred and he is Nigerian and can be no older than eighteen although he asserts that he's twenty-nine, perhaps because he knows that I am his senior. In fact, I am thirty-two. I met Wilfred in the emergency room. He suffered a minor head wound and claimed that he had been struck by a toaster-oven that was thrown out of a window on the rue Strasbourg St. Denis. This was an improbable story but I saw no particular reason to question him on it. I tended to him and as I did so, he told me about himself. I have to say that I was charmed by him straight away. Not only was he physically stunning, but he spoke with an accent I relish, an accent so much like butter to the ear. I must have encouraged him just for this. It didn't matter that I could hardly understand him. I live in France and have had French lovers although I hardly understand the whole of the language. It is better, I find, not to understand the languages of men. Then a woman is under fewer obligations and much freer of expectancy. For a woman, however, who seeks truths in her encounters and exchanges, I would not recommend this posture. She will be hotly disappointed with the world of men and women. I myself am, in fact, this sort of woman, and my greatest betrayal is this generalized deceit. Deceit breeds deceit and so on and so on. But I won't go on with this. I'm keeping to the lesser treacheries here.

Now I can't recall exactly how Wilfred managed to get

my number from me as, as a general rule, I don't give it out to my patients. It was very unprofessional to have done so with Wilfred, but I did it. I suppose I was feeling exceptionally lenient toward him, even maternal in a way. Although, no, it wasn't quite that. He inspired in me a feeling of protectiveness mitigated by another sentiment more matured, more carnal, desirous perhaps. There was something innocent yet alarmingly man-of-the-world about him. I was hardly guessing then, that he was seducing me, intentionally. It is often like this with me. I know nothing of these deliveries and am incapable at times, of both being seduced and seducing. Although both happen in spite of me.

My first appointment with Wilfred was at the Café Pompadour, a more or less smart bar, that he had chosen. It is the sort of place with finger-paint paintings in the primary color scheme hanging on the walls at varying heights. In one of the walls was a hole, made, one might guess, in the heat of a *bagarre*. We sat at a rickety wooden table and ordered drinks. Both of us were quiet and shy to speak. I was somewhat apprehensive and peeved at myself for having agreed to come and chastised myself for my lack of better judgment. But then the drinks came and the stifled atmosphere that had settled between the two of us lightened some. I asked him questions about Nigeria and he mentioned that he had an uncle who was a dentist. He also has a sister in Marseilles who is a cabaret singer. I asked him if he had many friends in Paris and he said,

"Ah no. I am here since one year and the Paris girls are not so easy-speak. And as a result I have fewer friends."

Telling me this was his prelude into more confidences.

"It is so unusual to meet someone as kind like you who takes care of my head and who speaks kinder and gives me her phone number. Most Paris girls are refusing to give the telephone number. They are all the time refusing and lying about those numbers."

And I am just like them, usually, I thought to myself. I was feeling quite foolish.

"What the Paris girl musts know but doesn't is that the Nigerian mens are strong ones. Blackmens are very strong and are satisfying the ladies. But maybe you know this. Sure. Do you make love with Blackmens?"

I found this talk bewildering and distasteful. This is the sort of thing I've always found absurd. Had he asked me, "Do you sleep with plumbers?" or "Do you sleep with cab drivers?" or "Do you sleep with dwarves?" it would have amounted to the same thing, nonsense. I made no comment but he continued.

"You are pretty and with all that blondy hair. And when I go to Nigeria for a week, I will take you with me. So this way you will see for one week where I was growing and living. Sure. And everything will be done for you and you will have a room with many casual-look pillows and a larger bed. Things will be very good to you in Nigeria. Sure."

I said nothing to encourage him. I said nothing at all. He was speaking an amorous code unfamiliar to me, a discourse that I could only have judged as hyperbolic and precocious. So I didn't judge it at all but finished my drink and suggested that we leave.

Between this meeting and the next, I went about my work as always only I felt myself falling prey to an excessive erotic curiosity that I could not dialogue with reasonably. I began to wonder at his hands, which were strong and sensual like those of a man who drives large manual vehicles for a living, a hand gripping the wheel and a deft hand on the shift. I thought of his mouth and his full lips that one could get lost in so pleasurably. And my curiosity led me where indeed it always does, into the arms of my conjured beloved. And so upon our second meeting, Wilfred and I became lovers.

We were lovers for several months and neither one of us was displeased. We were delighted with each other. I can understand why Wilfred sees this rupture as brutal and inexplicable. There was nothing wrong. We had remained desirous of one another throughout. I have been tempted to explain everything to him but have resisted. And I know this is best.

I claim responsibility for what happened. After all I am a nurse and have been trained by the medical establishment. I was careless in my methods and am now two months along. There is no question of my not keeping this child. I want it. But Wilfred will not know that he is a father. He is a child himself and has aspirations and things ahead of him to do. And really, I don't want that sort of attachment to him. It's just this way. So there is my betrayal. It's a functional and livable one, in the sense that it is allowing three people to live, imperfectly perhaps but freely. I will not judge it. It will be judge of itself in time.

• • •

Last weeks I was sadder and so much in chagrin that my bests girlfriend, the Nurse Lime-Away forgets me and is never speaking and seeing me. I wrote her a letter to tell her how I miss her and love her. I wrote this one:

Nurse Lime-Away, I really miss you terrible just the way I'm missing the Angels of God because you know, Nurse Lime-Away, I've never seen them and also the way I'm missing a chicken with horns. I've never seen them. If I were a rich man, I'd buy the Eiffel Tower for you and give it to you to be yours. But because it isn't so, and as a result it can't be so. But I think that when it will be so it will also be so.

But that Nurse Lime-Away was never responding to my epistle. And my calls neither. I was leaving those messages more and more. Plenty of them, often. Sure. And I tried to seem very ill so that it look like I had the sleeping sickness, so that I musts go to God's Hotel where she is working. So I go in and I'm making my complaint and pretending all that sleepiness. A nurse comes to fetch me. She's a blondy too, as Nurse Lime-Away but she is not pretty at all. Not at all. I think she's not really blondy. She's a false one and not an angel like Nurse Lime-Away who is always so kinder. This nurse puts me in a chair but I am every lying down and not sitting as she wants it, so sleepy and my eyes ever closing. So she is becoming terrible mad and thinks she isn't understanding me when I say, "The Nurse Lime-Away please." But I know she is all the time understanding and is just a wicked lady. And as a result I stand up to my feet and walkaway. But this blondy nurse is chasing after me with a needle and is yelling me to stop myself where I am. But I don't stop a minute and run out this giant door of God's Hotel where the Nurse Lime-Away is ever with sick mens and women and wickeder nurses.

So there have been many bad and lonelier days for me. And I thought of seeking council at the consultation office of the Professor Touré. He can bring back the loved one in four days. He can find lost affections. He can guarantee absolute fidelity. Sure. But as my father is a man, I am a man. And mens, if they are truer mens, do not consult the medium and pay for all those services and advisories. The truer mens put sticks in their mouths and grip them with the teeth, very harder. And what passes is what passes. And when their teeth loosen from the stick, they will know that they are ever living still and that this is a good thing. And so after several more days with a stick, I was better a bit and feeling quite alright. By this time, I am now sporting much more than starting from those days with the stick. Sure.

It was not long ago, then, that I was sitting in the café that I like bests and drinking that Carslberg beer. There were beauties all about me and I was feeling quite nice and trying to do my bests to find the good one. And I did not seek long for she was sitting at that table next to me, drinking a soda pop from the bottle itself. So she was not a Paris girl, this is true. Because the Paris girl is always drinking from a glass and never like this one. I turn myself near the right so that I'm looking at her and I ask, "Do you have the time, please?" She is looking surprising and replies me, "five thirty." I thank her and drink again. Then I say to her, "My friend who was coming is detaining. Would you like to join this table? I would be most happy to fetch you another of those soda pops." She did take a time to agree to this but she was agreeing at last.

It was like this that I was knowing Hilda-Lucía Jurmando de Queiroz, a Copacabana girl. Hilda-Lucía is most beautiful in a red dress just fitting her closer and closer. She wears her hair in many braids with many hair extensions and as a result they are long as licorice ropes. She looks like a Nigerian girl from the capital city but she is a Copacabana one instead.

Things were quite alright with Hilda-Lucía. She is a part-time in a perfume shop by the name Chez Mafleur and is very handy with sprays. So it isn't easy to go to Chez Mafleur and leave there later without some spray scent on you. One musts like this or one musts not enter. It is this way. Hilda-Lucía always is smelling lovelier and all her jewelries are gold. She is often saying that her great fortune is that she is knowing the owner, Pépé Cohen, and so she can be a part-time there. And her apartment where we go for intimates is wealthier, like the residence of a life president indeed. This man, Pépé Cohen, is one man of international jet-set, owning luxury-items chain stores and banks in the world around. Hilda-Lucía was an entertainment maid in his mansion residence in Copacabana, where there were ever parties so full of glory and wealthier mens and their ladies in finery. Hilda-Lucía has told me some of this so that it has been seen in my ear's eye. And she musts wear a uniform to serve and please all those jet-sets, and she was so beautiful even in the uniforms and making those jealousies, that Pépé Cohen was sending her to Paris city with so many benefits and never forgetting the instructives. I asked Hilda Lucía if Pépé Cohen could give me some helpful too, for finding a job in this opportunity town. And she said, no, she didn't think so. I asked her for a key to her palace apartment and this she was refusing also, like Nurse Lime-Away who had only the one key and keeping it by herself.

I only visit the palace apartment with the consenting invitation of Hilda-Lucía. I enjoy escorting her to those greenery parks near the Eiffel Tower, and find myself doing more and nearly as the Frenchmens with all those romantics and preliminaries. Hilda-Lucía is much appreciating this and isn't refusing me when I call for seeing her, except once when she was belly-aching like the ladies sometimes do. I was sending some bouquet flowers to her in hopes she's feeling better and alright. This is what the Frenchmens do and I'm thinking it's the right one. When I go to see her the next day, there aren't the bouquet flowers I was sending her. They aren't there at all. I asked her if she received them well and she was denying this reception. Saying all the time that no flowers were delivered but she was thanking me for my intentions all the same. But when I was leaving that apartment kingdom, I saw the concierge and he was taking out the garbages and in these garbages were the sweet bouquet flowers I was sending to Hilda-Lucía. And they were fresh and beautiful as ever and I knew she was not putting them in the garbages because they weren't beautiful enough. She was doing this for other reasons.

Then it just being another time in that palace apartment, the doorbell rang and two mens are entering with a flower bouquet five times the size of the one I was sending. There were even flowers from my Nigeria country. Never was I seeing before so grander bouquet flowers. Hilda-Lucía was ever delighting with this one and touching it softer with the tip of her fingers and at much admiration. Then there was a card on a ribbon and she took it and was reading it but there was only one word on it and this word was "Pépé." I was knowing this because Hilda-Lucía hazardly dropped the card and I was speedy to pick up. As a result I was seeing it all. I wasn't saying those things I was thinking to Hilda-Lucía but I was great wondering at her. I was wondering at those Copacabana girls and thinking that maybe they weren't the good family ones or else they're just too pretty for God and mens to make understanding with. I know that I am not the same man as Pépé Cohen with so many wealths and golden things and gianty bouquet flowers that are ever impressing the ladies. But my father, the Professor Touré, is a wise man and wisdoms are like gold and worthy of more. Sure. I am becoming as my father, just my wisdom is to be a computer scientist of prestige and higher calibers. And so one day I will say to my fairer lady, "You musts be thinking that I am the most intelligent man you are knowing." And she will say, "Sure."

Hilda-Lucía likes very much to dance with a partner or a hula hoop. Sometimes when I go to the palace apartment the high-tech hi-fi, the one I am always programming for her, is at the full blasts. It just being Copacabana music. And when I come in, she is dropping the hula hoop and pulling me to her closer so that together we are pressing and doing the lover dance. Hilda-Lucía is always smelling like a garden delight only more pleasurable to love with because she is an exquisite dancing girl.

It was happening one day, that we were dancing as if we were doing the other sweet thing when we are hearing keys in the door lock. We didn't have time to disengage enough before a small, baldy man in a smoking suit was walking in like the palace apartment was belonging to him with property rights. And it was belonging to him. This little man just being Pépé Cohen. Hilda-Lucía was declaring, "Pépé!" and disengaging from my arms and legs. "Pépé!" Then they were speaking in that Copacabana tongue, furious and angrier, both of those two. Pépé was yelling at me too and pointing his fingers at me like a little gun and I was thinking he musts in truth have one of these in his trouser as those gangster mens are always keeping them. And so I was wanting to leave terrible but was also fearing for Hilda-Lucía and for her good safety I didn't leave but was staying. I was putting myself in front of Hilda for shield protection and all this time they were screaming to and fro louder and louder and I was not understanding any of their tongue but only that it was just an angrier one than I was ever hearing before. That little wealthy man, Pépé Cohen, had a reddy face like the whitemens do when there is trouble inside them, in the blood. Then he was yelling something in a higher voice, something, perhaps a question. And Hilda-Lucía with her voice now down and calm answered him. The following episode was that Hilda-Lucía was moving away from behind me so that she and Pépé Cohen were together turning at me and looking at me with terrible hostilities. And I was understanding that Hilda is preferring the wealths to the loves and that she wickeder even than the nurse with the needle at the God's Hotel and that I musts escape from this palace apartment. But they were together standing before the door to blockade it from my departure. And all this time I was ever thinking that Pépé Cohen had this little Copacabana gun in his trouser and that his liability to do away with me was greater. Sure. And so more carefully I was speaking to him. I was just saying polite, "Mister Cohen, I would be obliged to leave at this moment." But that little jet-set was looking at me vicious as a mad dog and he was replying was, "I kill you." And he was holding his hands out like he was having it around my neck and shaking.

So I was understanding then, that he wasn't employing a gun but was going to attempt my murder with those two hands. And so I was feeling alright. I was taking the hula hoop quick and throwing it around those two money lovers together. Then I was making them spin and spin in so many circles, it just leaving them too dizzy and making them lose their places. I exited that door and was leaving speedy that apartment kingdom, never coming back again. Ever and ever. Sure.

• • •

Stanley and I celebrated our first-year anniversary with a moonlight boat ride down the Marne. One would hardly guess Stanley to be a sentimental man from the looks of him; he's of Bunyan stature, has a deliberate jaw, and might appear taciturn or somewhat feral to those who don't know him, but he is very warm hearted and quite a romantic at that. All evening long he addressed me as Nurse Lime-Away as he once had when he was broken limbed and in traction at the Hôtel Dieu. This is a spoony game of his. With his head in my lap, he looked up at me and said, "Nurse Lime-Away, you are my angel of mercy." I called him a fool which he is indeed when he acts this way.

Stanley is, or rather was, a professional rugby player. He was en route back from a game in Bordeaux when, having gotten as far as Paris, he was so rudely injured in an automobile accident and sent to the Hôtel Dieu to be repaired. He stayed with us a month and during this time we came to know each other as I was the only nurse who could communicate with him beyond gestures and yes and no. He spoke no French then. We visited every day, although only for short spells, when I did my rounds. He'd ask me sometimes to read him a poem from a book of his. In fact they were limericks and I got to liking them. Then I began to have tea with him at four o'clock when I took my afternoon pause. I read to him from a book of his called *I've Tasted the Crime,* a detective novel of sorts.

By the time Stanley was about to leave, my pregnancy was showing, which must have been why he thought I was married. On the day he checked out he gave me two tickets to a rugby game for "you and your husband" as a gesture of thanks. I wished him the best and bid him good-bye.

I ended up going to that game alone, as I couldn't find anyone who wanted to come along on the other ticket. I found my seat and spotted Stanley right away. He was two tiers below talking to some men in hats. I called down to him and he seemed quite happy to see me. He came up to where I was to say hello and seeing that I was alone asked me if my husband had decided not to come. I told him there very simply that I wasn't married and that I hadn't been able to find anyone else, my friends being out of town or engaged in some way. He suggested that I come down and join him. I did.

This outing led to many others and although I didn't care to notice, I was spending a great deal of my free time with him. I was being led without bothering to know it. And Stanley, in his blind and dégagé manner, was leading me to love him. I never think of asking questions when I am busy with someone. I was very busy with Stanley. And then I assumed that my pregnancy made me undesirable or perhaps off-limits. But I was wrong. Underneath my assumptions and my never-asked questions there was something else at work. Because when, after several months of knowing each other, Stanley asked me to marry him, I said yes without a hesitation.

Throughout my pregnancy, Stanley was very supportive. The closer the time came to delivering, the more involved he became in the event, as if he were the father. And now, if someone were to remind me that Stanley wasn't the blood father, although nobody has done this as it must be obvious judging from little Wilma's color that he isn't, my reaction might be to vehemently deny this, so wholly has he adopted her as his own. Even I forget.

· · ·

The day before yesterday, my father, the Professor Touré, was paying me the higher regards, with many compliments on my successes in the scholastic field.

"My son," he was saying to me, "your first year at the Paris University of Mathematics and Informatic Science has been a brilliant one. Your performance has been pleasing your father and the faculty as well. For this you have the full-paying scholarship which will make you most comfortable during your studies. I congratulate you. You have become a man in this passing year. And as all true mens, you have proved yourself to your father in many ways. You have made yourself successful in his honor. But do be careful son, it would not be so wise an idea to sire more children before you have a wife wearing your lawful ring. This I am warning you."

I was listening to all those compliments upon me so that I almost wasn't hearing my father's last surprising mention. But in truth, I did hear it. But then once I heard it, I wasn't believing it.

"What are you saying Father?" I was asking him. "I am a man, sure, but I'm never a father yet!"

"It happens often and sometimes," my father went on, "that a man doesn't know the whereabouts of his loin fruit, this being the fault of women. God made some women too quiet and others too loud. But yes, a women who tends the sick has given birth to your child in common. And I am telling you that many young mens are doing these things that you are doing. In our Nigeria country the mens must marry the pregnant girl in all honor and receiving that kind bank note from her father. But in this country, it is strict and important for a man to be a strong one with more and more money at the Commercial Bank and fewer children to eat all those funds to deficits. You are living in this country and must do as the mens here. You are a new, continental Nigerian man and your life in Paris City will be grander and grander. Just be watching peaceful those ladies who are always so beautiful. Take all those modern precautions and do not worry your fatherhood at this time, my son. One day, when you are wearing that navy blue suit and walking into those banks with the staffs bowing at you and calling you the "Sir," you will have that wife and childrens that you recognize too and who do your bidding. Sure."

I left my father's premises with very many shock thoughts and confusions. I was trying to think myself the father of Nurse Lime-Away's child. I was telling myself and not believing yet. But by the night time I believed and was trying to find ways to have a correspondence with the Nurse Lime-Away who was always refusing those calls and epistles. I was hearing my father alright. He was telling me to have no worries about this. He is a wise man certainly with plentiful sage councils and I was knowing that he was right. But all of these wisdoms could not detain me from making my beseech and claiming myself father of that baby that the Nurse Lime-Away was so quietly bringing into this world.

So I was just sitting down at my study desk to write her an epistle to tell her what is in my heart and mind. I was doing this only for preliminaries—until I was thinking of better plans. But I did not needs to think of plan B because two days after sending that letter I was receiving a call from the Nurse Lime-Away who was losing her breaths and asking to meet me as soon as possible. So I made her an appointment for the day following.

The Nurse Lime-Away was prettier than always and in her white, slim-waist dress that I was remembering so well with fondness. She greeted me in the Frenchmen's way with kissing on both cheeks. She was upmost nervous though and was pulling at those goldie locks. She was asking me how I was knowing that she had a child by me, and I was answering that it mattered so little how I was knowing but that I was knowing and was there to beseech and claim my offspring. Then that pretty Nurse Lime-Away took to weeping. Oh she wept and wept and cried and wept another time. So everything was wet after her torrent and her nose and eyes were reddy. She was speaking with much difficulties and was explaining that she was married to a man she loved and that this man had adopted her daughter. He was, moreover, according to legal writ, her father. Then she was weeping once more with greater chagrins. So I was telling her, "This man that is your husband is looking like he is the father in the eyes of law-mens. But never be forgetting that I am the father by the rights of blood."

Suddenly the Nurse Lime-Away stopped this tearfall and was blowing her nose into a white kleenex tissue as if she was blowing out an idea right there.

"Yes," she was saying. "My husband is the legal father. But then this could only make you the godfather."

I was not so sure about this godfather name. I wasn't knowing it's meaning exact but this father title was sounding all prestige in my ears, with such a holy preface. And so I was asking her to tell me with all due precisions the meaning of such a title. Because in my Nigeria country, there can only be one father, never counting two.

And so she was explaining to me that the godfather is a spiritual guideman who is ever giving wisdoms to his child and always hallmarking his birthday with appropriate gifts, and the primary holy days as well. I was telling her I

88

knew nothing of holy days and she was replying that she would be making a list of them for me. I looked at the Nurse Lime-Away and was thinking to myself that it was a terrible pity for a mother being so sad because these chagrins stricken the baby and make for bad blood all around and everywhere in those concerned. And then it was the truth that I was not loving the Nurse Lime-Away as before I had, and she belonging to another man, this is alright. Sure. Besides this much, I am now almost in love with my new Paris girlfriend, Rhonda.

And so I was agreeing to act as this godfather title, insisting that she get me those lists of the holy days speedy. She said yes and was telling me that I musts soon be attending the holy baptism, which is the official ceremony of the godfathers. I was replying that it was always my pleasure.

I was leaving the Nurse Lime-Away with a feeling of greater relief that I was the appointed official godfather and not the official law father. This will mean that I can continue my successes in bachelor ease only never forgetting to impart pithies on the child, from time to time on those holy days.

In truth my father, the Professor Touré, is always right, and as he insists that I musts do as these continental Frenchmens so I am doing with much dedication to wisdoms and wealths.

Now it is the summertime and this Paris city is ever flocking with scanty sundresses and much park-time amusements. With Rhonda and others, taking all those precautions. All around this opportunity town. Sure.

Testimony

When Father Perro found he could give himself pleasure he was fourteen years old. This happened in a tree house. At that time of course, he wasn't yet Father Perro. He was just Juaquin Perro, Jr. And as for what exactly happened in the little tree house off the Calle Virgen de la Paz no one can say, although one can imagine easily enough. Father Perro knew pleasure at fourteen and it was, as he had always feared, at the tip of his fingertips. Had he been told that one in the hand wasn't worth two in the bush he would have wept. A sorry man. For he was ordained at eighteen and, for his own sake, pleaded chaste on a stump in Los Baños at eighteen and a half. Yes, Juaquin Perro, Jr., had chosen a life of difficulty and bore the title "Father" austerely.

Father Perro was secretly in love, though, with an exquisite young man named Rocco. Rocco was the seminary gardener. He mowed the lawn bare chested and wore such tight trousers that his panty lines showed. Rocco was virile and thewy and once when he was bending over pruning roses, Father Perro noticed a tag jutting out from his pants. It read the letter "L," which made the father dizzy and suddenly embarrassed. He chastised himself for this curiosity and lay in bed that night tormented by improper dreams. Although in the morning he recognized these devilish struggles as the very difficulty he had chosen and so embraced them.

When he learned that Rocco was an orphan and a heathen, his desire was rerouted and directed toward converting the beloved. Often Father Perro would avidly recount the parables of Christ as Rocco hoed the vegetable garden or fertilized the seminary green. Rocco didn't listen though and perhaps would have considered the priest a nuisance had he noticed him at all. But Rocco was a concrete man, a hands-on man. He reckoned a story a lie. He had never bothered with the multiplication tables. But he had learned the facts of life early on. The facts he held on to. When he was handed his paycheck by the acolyte Diamando, that was a fact. When he lay with the funambulist Melodina in her camper and buried his head in her breasts, that too was a fact. Anything his hands touched and cared to remember was a fact. To him a fact was a fact.

As time went on, Father Perro began to grow impatient with Rocco's indifference to Christ's love and to his own helpless desire and one day in utter exasperation he questioned the gardener in the rose garden.

"Do you not see, Rocco, that you are no longer an orphan, that you have a brother in Jesus and a father in his Father? Do you not see this? Do you not feel their love?"

Rocco, who had been on his knees straightening a fallen rose bush, stood up, looking at Father Perro deliberately for the first time. And the priest was haggard then and teary eyed. Desperate, desperate. Rocco ran a hand through his thick brown hair and leaned back on his left leg. He spoke slowly and with an accent unfamiliar to Father Perro. It was, in fact, a Turkish accent, but Father Perro never knew this.

"No," he said, "I do not see. I don't see but you here. And you are not my brother. And you are not my father."

"No. This is true. But I am testimony, Rocco. I am testimony!"

Father Perro was excited and sputtering. He could not contain himself and so was consumed by a relentless passion and spoke till he nearly lost his own wind and flailed his arms and fell down on his knees onto a sprig of thorns. And while he was being so consumed, Rocco went back to his work and eventually left for the toolshed to fetch a watering bucket. When he came back to the rose garden, he found the priest slumped on a bench asleep. He tapped him on the shoulder and said, "Wake up you," and left him before he regained consciousness.

Father Perro fell prey to a morbid drowsiness in the weeks following this episode. He gave listless homilies and petitioned for the souls of the orphaned. Much of the time he lay on a cot and thought of nothing. Or if he could muster the strength, he would try to invoke the Holy

Ghost with two sticks. And all the while he would say to himself, "This is my difficulty and I cannot forsake it." He passed out several times too.

Then one morning a thought finally did come to him, and it was as if a divine gift had been set on his temple. Its coming coincided with the acolyte's excessive ringing of the chapel bells after a wedding. Hearing them, he sat upright on the cot abruptly awoken from his somnolence, and the idea was so limpid, so assured in his mind that he laughed to himself. A hoarse laugh and the first one in weeks. "I will ring him up. Yes, I will ring him today. I will call the man from the rectory phone booth. He chooses to neither hear nor see me on the seminary green but the phone he will answer. He will hear me on the phone."

And so it went that Father Perro began calling Rocco regularly in the evenings after five o'clock mass while still in frock. This ritual (for it did become a rite of sorts) began and ended with the same question each time.

"This is Father Perro," he would say, "Have you gone to church today?"

"I do not know you. I do not know Father Perro. If you call again, I hurt you. I could break Father Perro's mouth that is talking."

But Father Perro continued to call nightly although during the day he diligently avoided Rocco. For he was in truth deeply frightened by the gardener's menaces. He spent his days in a blind funk, hiding behind pillars and the shadows of other men's robes. He did not recover possession of himself until the evening, after having set the host on the tongues of wealthy matrons. That was the one moment of the day when the flocks came to him and took with the mouth what he was ordained to hold in the hand. But that moment came and went too quickly and meant so little really, compared to his beloved, compared to the first word he uttered when the father rang him. That word was yes. "Yes?" was what Rocco said when he picked up the phone. It was both question and answer and the joy of Father Perro's day. It was his peculiar epiphany and his supper too, the manifestation of an ultimate love. The love of his brother. Sometimes when he called he heard feminine giggles and was happy to be disturbing an intimate meeting in which he could not partake. Melodina, after a grueling day on the rope, was amused by these calls in the beginning. But then seeing how they put Rocco in the foulest moods and made his loving too rugged and self-serving, she began to dislike them as much as he. Sometimes he could not even be a man to her. Before he was her camper gentleman, the smoothest of lovers, the highlight of her day and she would sprawl for him with pleasure, but since the advent of the calls, she found herself sharing him with a bogy. She perhaps grew jealous. In any case she cut her hair very short.

Father Perro had indeed become something of a specter, not only to the two lovers but unto himself as well. He lost his appetite and ate only a can of sardines at noontime with four saltine crackers. And this he did because of a lingering sense of duty for he was never hungry. He continued to do what was expected of him at the seminary, only he moved about so inconspicuously that he was hardly noticed. It has not yet been said that Father Perro was bald. However he was. Yet when he stood upon the altar, his head no longer shone, primitive and solid as an egg. There was a translucent and absent quality to his face. In the confessional, his confessors received the same meager penance regardless of the gravity of the sin at hand. Father Perro lost all taste for the penitential. He was lackluster and breathless. One parishioner, a widow who had been grieving her husband's death, swore that when Father Perro paid a sympathy visit and reached out to pat her shoulder, his hand went straight through her breast. "Through to the bone," she told everyone, "I saw his hand go in and felt his fingers rap on my bone." Not many believed her but some did. Most didn't care to take an interest in the priest. He was odorless. Although he did swing the censer in procession. He was bland and would have tasted like a communion wafer had you licked his cheek.

One morning while putting on his sneakers, Father Perro suddenly lost sight of his right foot. That is to say, he simply could not see it. And when he grabbed where it should have been, he pulled at the carpet instead and ended up with a cockroach between his fingers. "My God! My God!," he cried, "You have taken my right foot. You have taken the good foot for your holy purposes. May it serve you well. I was once a whole-limbed man. Now I am gimpy." With that he genuflected, stood up again and in a daze walked over to his sink. When he reached the sink, he slowly took two steps backward and one forward, aware suddenly that his walking was in no way impaired. Both feet were there although one of them was nowhere to be seen. Father Perro decided then to let out the hem of his robe. To others Father Perro appeared the same as always, if a bit scruffier. No one cared in the least. That night,

Father Perro made his call to Rocco, whose threats had become increasingly violent and nonsensical.

"Man," he said vehemently, "I kill you. I kill Father Perro with the two finger."

This pleased the priest and made him tremble, and tremble again so that his innards were troubled. He was certain that he had shaken the gardener's indifference. As he listened to his stomach growl in bed that night, he imagined the wall before him tumbling down and on the other side of it, Rocco, exposed and vulnerable as a lamb. Yes, Rocco was the fleecy lamb and he, the shepherd. "Provide me, Oh Lord," he said in his prayers, "with the staff so that I may lead the lost one back to your almighty kingdom. He knows only the sweetness of almond candies and the perfume of a tightrope walker. He has yet to taste the goodness of your pastures."

When Father Perro got up the next morning, he stood on two feet he could not see. Also, his left arm was missing. He was dismayed and began to worry that now he would not escape notice, that he would be found out and subjected to an exorcism by Bishop Trujillo, a specialist in demonology. As for Father Perro himself, he believed in the seen and the unseen. The less he saw, the more firmly he believed in the Presence. This was faith. The others, if they honored the credo, would see in him the design of divine workings. Such were his thoughts. He said a five-minute rosary and went about the day, footless and empty sleeved.

Much to his amazement however, nobody remarked this absence of limbs. He was treated the same as always by peers and parishioners and elicited no particular reflection. "Oh, they are cruel," he thought to himself. "They see that I am testimony and pretend that this isn't so. They are cowards and hypocrites. They claim to believe in the unseen and yet when the unseen is held before their eyes they feign blindness."

Father Perro was hurt, then angry, here belligerent, there haughty. And each morning as he rose from his bed, he found that some new part of him had disappeared in the night. The erasure was accomplished over a forty-day period during which the priest became a malignant and provocative figure at the seminary. He was hardly adored as he thought he deserved to be. Rather, he was often reprimanded by Bishop Trujillo and sent looks of disapprobation by the other clergy as he did behave wickedly. Once, while passing out Holy Communion, he stuck his entire fist in the mouth of a mariachi named Paco Rojo. The poor man gagged and took the host down the wind pipe. After this happened, Father Perro was docked and put on a rigorous regime of penance and unleavened crackers. "I'm not a Jew," he would say when Brother Jorge brought him a tray of water and Matzoh crackers. "I am testimony." He wasn't listened to, though, and eventually he was left to his confinement and forgotten. On the fortieth day Father Perro went to wash in the sink and discovered, when he looked in the mirror, that his face had been taken too. He had always been quite fond of looking at his head in the mirror and so was saddened by its absence. It was terribly hard to bear. Yes, there was much difficulty in that. Yet difficulty was his vocation and he simply said to the Lord, "May you make good use of that head. It's not such a bad one. Amen." Father Perro then went over to his wardrobe to get a frock. But at that moment, as his hand took the hanger, he realized, dropping his arm and laughing to himself, that there was no need for him to dress. He was after all, entirely invisible. A striking disclosure! Father Perro clicked his heels in tribute to the supernatural agency's merry-making and was elated. He waltzed about his room, doing three pirouettes, then a gruesome plié. It had been so long since he had danced. He was raw and flabby. He was flat-footed too. But what joy! He opened his window and leaped out of it into a tulip bed. Again he was in the garden after months of avoiding it for fear of his beloved. But he was fearless now and beyond all difficulty. He was in the blessed garden.

That same morning, Rocco was clipping an ornamental lemon tree with a pair of shears. He had been in a treacherous mood of late, having lost his Melodina to a dentist named Richardson, who, in an effort to make peace, had offered him a free consultation. Rocco was a man of pride and refused. He accused Melodina of taking up with the dentist Richardson because he was American and had a house with seven bathrooms and seven TVs. "You look at the seven TV . . . You sit on the seven toilet. Then you are bored and come to me," he warned her. But Melodina apparently liked the continental comforts and abandoned the camper for good. Besides, the dentist Richardson was training her to be his dental hygienist. She was a smart girl.

Throughout all this, Rocco had continued to receive Father Perro's calls, these calls that he held responsible for the unfortunate turn of events. Because of these calls, he had become less of a man. A lesser man with difficulty answering that calling, the one which most young men rose to answer without question at the snap of a brassiere. Rocco was driven to a seemingly incurable insomnia and impotence. He was on edge and watched his boundaries carefully. He drew a mental circle around his person and kept himself for himself.

Now, it was as he was trimming the lemon tree that morning that he heard his name being called from behind. "Rocco, my brother. I have led you to his pasture. Let us eat the fruits."

He recognized the voice surely enough and turned around to see the naked Father Perro running toward him, arms akimbo and eyes crazed. The priest was calling him "brother" and his withered genitals romped as he jumped over garden pews and begonia urns. He was upon Rocco sooner than either of the two could have expected. And Rocco who was quicker with the hand than the feet, held the two-fingered shears out so that when Father Perro made the final leap to his beloved's breast, he took instead the two fingers into his heart. And for a while in the garden, Rocco held him and cradled his head until the two fingers had clipped the last of the heart strings.

A week later, the clergy began to wonder where Father Perro had gone. One suggested that he might have left to visit his stepsister, Mathilda, in Bolivia. Another thought he might have gone on a fishing trip. When two weeks later there was still no sign of him, a police report was made by Bishop Trujillo's secretary, Juana Lalinda. Then it was forgotten about. His room was eventually given to an Argentinian novitiate.

Rocco had buried Father Perro in the rose garden and put a birdbath statue of the Virgen de la Paz over the spot. No one ever knew. There were of course no witnesses. There could be no testimony.

The Blue Suit

*I*t was on the eve of Easter that the little violet lovebird of Cécile Misouris choked on a chick pea and died. Easter morning Cécile Misouris awoke to a silence she hardly heard. It was an indifferent one, of the kind that might herald an event, or a prospect, perhaps even a migration. Indeed something had come and gone in the night in the utility apartment of Cécile Misouris. The silence was an afterthought. She opened her eyes to it, then she adjusted quickly.

Cécile had lovely brown eyes, somewhat bovine and, in the morning, very sweet to look at. But there was no one to notice them that morning. She lifted her arms over her head, slid her fanny down toward her feet, and stretched in bed. She thought of the day ahead of her. She would put on her blue suit. That is to say her Sunday best. Yes, her Easter jubilee, the suit she had found in a box behind the Galéries Lafayette. There had been a blood stain on it but she washed it meticulously and it came clean. Sometimes when she did think about that stain she cried. She couldn't fathom it but emotionally. Underneath she would put on the pretty lingerie she purchased at the flea market. All of it silk and some of it ravaged. The coquette! For Easter mass, yes, for the Resurrection of the Savior she would do this. And she thought of Monsieur Bretonnier, the widower layman, and of how afterwards he would take her to that piquant bar à vins for tasty counter fare and then whisk her off to his pavillion in the woods. "Not many young ladies are as lucky as I," she often told herself. Other than this, she was a maid for a Madame X.

Cécile spent the first moments of the silence reorganizing herself mentally. In other words, she chattered. And could not be bothered by afterthoughts. Although they were giving her ample warning. The mere absence of feather ruffle and chirp bespoke it. She chose, like so many of her generation and caste, to adhere to clutter. So she heard herself and not the had-happened. But then again this didn't matter for what was inevitable was equally indelible. Her fate was spotted.

Once out of bed, the first thing Cécile Misouris did Easter morning, as she did every morning, was go over to the window to open the blinds. Only when she got to the window and to the cage that sat on the ledge, she saw that her little violet lovebird was not on his swing but lying motionless on the floor of the cage. "Oh God," she supplicated, "let it not be true. Let it be that he has only fainted". She then picked him up and held him in her palm. "But he is as cold and as stiff as a cobblestone. Ah!

The violet bird is dead! Mon petit Violet est mort!" She wept. And when she saw that lodged in his narrow throat was a chick pea, the very one she had taken from her couscous and given him as a snack treat the evening before, she wept bitterly. With unrelenting tears of remorse and guilt she cried. She thought of his suffering, he who had been the joy at her window and the loveliest of chimes. The little one who so artfully picked at her nose. And this because of a false expectation and a desire to please, so poorly contrived, so misconstrued. Who had told her that the bird relished the chick pea? She had thought it up herself. And now the clarity of the afterthought. The tiny dead fellow in the palm of her hand. How clear and hard it all was indeed. She hadn't seen it happen and yet it had happened! So much was like this for Cécile. Sometimes she missed the bus and even though she did not see the bus she had missed pull away, she knew that she had missed it all the same. There was not a bone of the Doubting Thomas in her. She had not been a brilliant student in catechism, but what she had learned was heartfelt and believed. And so when she fell to her knees, the bird in her fist, to pray for the soul of the departed, she suddenly stopped herself. And remembered something. The words of Soeur Josianne or perhaps those of Père Frédérique, that adamant discourse on the division of souls. How simply it had been spelled out: Man had one and Animal did not. Even the flying friar, Joseph of Copertino and St. Francis of Assisi whose affinity with birds and animals was keen and mystic, did not say, "The soul of the beast is!" So who was Cécile to say differently? She was a nobody's nobody. She lived in a maid's room and shared a hall toilet with six others. No, Cécile took dogma on its word and was left with small recourse from her pain. She looked toward delightful Jesus who had risen from the dead that very day but lost all courage and voice. She looked toward the Virgin Mary, mother of burden and sorrow but shied away ashamed. She turned toward Saint Teresa of Avila and was horrified. There was no help to be found. None of the holies availed themselves. Cécile could not even allow them to read her heart for her heart was in the wrong. She so desired to pray for the bird's safekeeping in limbo but could not. She was not a heretic. She suffered in keeping with the saints.

By the time Cécile regained some composure, she had already missed mass and Monsieur Bretonnier too. She would have to take care of Violet anyway. She looked lovingly at him and shed a few more tears. Then she picked him up and rubbed his soft downy body against her cheek for the last time. She carefully put him in a clean bath mitten. Then she thought of what to do next. "Now I will have to bury him somewhere. This is alright. Animals can be buried. I've heard it said. I've even seen it done." She decided on the Luxembourg Gardens where she often went on the warmer days to read her "Que Sais-Je?" and once dressed, left to catch the bus. Violet was in the mitten in her knapsack when she got on the bus. She took a window seat and held her package carefully on her lap. She was feeling very heavyhearted and weepy. Several stops down the route, a bearded dwarf got on the bus and sat next to her. "Ah," she said to herself, "another miserable one." But she paid little attention to him. She blew her nose and dried a tear here and there. When the bus reached her stop, the dwarf stood up to let her pass and then followed her out. She walked alongside the Faculté de Médecine and so did he. She walked up the stairs at the rue Antoine du Bois and so did he. She walked up the rue Monsieur Le Prince and so did he. Then, still a step behind her, he reached out and pulled at the hem of the blue suit. Cécile felt the tug and turned around with her hand raised to slap the culprit, which she imagined to be a dog. But she saw the dwarf there instead and lowered her hand.

"What are you doing?" she asked him indignantly.

"Mademoiselle, I have been following you on the right side. Walking and looking to dexter side. Three paws on ground and dexter forepaw raised. May I come along? May I come along some more? It would be my pleasure."

"No. There are things I must tend to. I haven't the time for company."

"Well then, I will do them with you. No! I will do them for you. Let me do them! Rumpelstiltskin was an evil good-doer, but I am a jack-of-all-trades and a lucky chap at that. I have helped many a damsel with a tribulation. And free of cost! I'm no snaky usurer. Me, Dandie-Lamb! Ho! Ho! Have dandy, will lambsy! Feed a Dan, starve a lamb! You've heard it, Love. Now, say. What's in the bag, my lady in waiting? Now, I'm waiting on you. Me, Dandie-Lamb!"

Had Cécile not been in a state of mourning she would have found this little man repugnant and his outburst offensive. But as it was she was vulnerable and therefore susceptible to him. She hugged her knapsack and said, "In this bag is my bird, Violet. He choked on a chick pea last night and died. I'm going to bury him in the park."

"Ah! But Mademoiselle, one cannot bury a tic or a tac in that park. You will be caught and taken to a hirsute magistrate who will heavily fine you or, worse, take pleasure in your graces and make of you a law lassie. Trust Dandie-Lamb. He is master of recesses, the cubby and the cunette. He'll molly the plot. He'll undertake the undertaker and spitchcock the chirper. Follow along. He, Dandie-Lamb!"

"Very well, then. Let's go quickly. I am distraught and cannot pray for the soul of the departed who doesn't have a soul. Although my heart is broken. Neither Jesus nor Mary nor Teresa of Avila will be invoked with the prayer cards. Let's go now and bury the bird."

So Cécile followed behind the dwarf up the street into the park. He waddled sprightly and she found herself skipping from time to time to keep up. He led her through a gate she hadn't known existed. It was the employees' entrance she supposed. They walked along a narrow cobblestone path with heavy shrubbery on either side. The foliage was still damp with morning dew. Cécile held her hands in front of her face to protect it from jutting twigs. They went on until they came to another gate. This time, a locked one. Dandie-Lamb took from around his ear a key that he kept hanging there and unlocked the gate. He pushed it open with his stumpy leg and bowing gallantly said to Cécile, "After you, my cherry Miss." She walked in with the trust of a mourner, although she did have to duck her head to get through. This should have perhaps made her apprehensive but did not. She walked into what appeared to be an enclosed garden, the walls of which were draped in ivy and morning glory vines. Iris and jonquils grew wildly around a cracked statue of the mischievous Pan and viola blanketed the ground above the graves. For this was a cemetery of sorts. Hundreds of miniature crosses made of sticks poked up from the soil. Most were merely two inches high. The tallest may have measured five inches. Cécile looked bewilderedly about her and said to herself, "If this must be done, then it must be done." Dandie-Lamb was tapping the ground with his left foot as if looking for something.

"Here we are then," he said. "Now let's have a look at the little fetid fellow for the estimate."

Cécile gently pulled Violet from the mitten and set him on the dwarf's outstretched hand.

"He's a popper alright! A smit of a smudge! Take five inches in depth and three in width. Tally ho! Chop chop, Clementine!"

With this he opened his knapsack and took out a trowel, a loin cloth, and salt and pepper shakers. He put the bird in the loin cloth and tied the two ends of it tightly. Then he started to dig. He dug avidly, whistling a peasant tune all the while. And when he was done, he wiped his brow like a man who had toiled. Yes, he had labored there and was to collect his livelihood too. That is to say, he reached into his pocket, pulled out a flask and took a long swig from it. "Aye," he said out loud to himself, "Work the mattock and be rewarded so justly." In the next few moments, however, a change came over him. His jocular countenance sobered and his ruddy face paled. He began to hum in the most monotone manner. He doused the bird with salt. He doused the bird with pepper. And meanwhile his solemn hum became a chant, a gibberish that Cécile couldn't understand nor cared to. She was content to let it babble in her ear. She was unharmed. Although the mantra had a lulling quality that made her sleepy. Yes, very sleepy indeed. This somnolence was remarkably potent, quicker than any fear it, and so seductive not a yawn contested. Cécile closed her sweet eyes, laid her head down in the Johnny-jump-ups and fell asleep. She slept heavily.

In her sleep she had a dream. She dreamed her unkempt hair was piled terrifically high on top of her head. This extravagant bun was in truth a nest with bits of grass and telephone wire and gum wrappers intertwined in it. And in the nest, sitting like a prince of peace, was Violet. Yes, that precious light of her mornings. Her beloved birdie! She was overjoyed to find him there in her hair and clapped her hands. Then the dream flashed to the house of Madame X who was to have a luncheon. Cécile was in the kitchen arranging petit fours on a silver, tiered tray. As she did so Violet flitted gaily about the kitchen. Suddenly the pastry chef burst in with a tray of pie crusts in his arms.

"Why in the world is the bird in the curd?" he exclaimed. Indeed, Violet had landed in a bowl of lemon curd and was stuck a bit. Cécile picked him up and put him back on her head.

"The bird has heard. Now he furrows in the burrow." Next the linen maid came in. She saw the preposterous coiffure and exclaimed, "I've heard of a bird flying over the herd but one in the hair is quite a scare!"

Cécile patted her bun and replied, "He's the poppet in the socket. He's the Bourbon of the turban."

Then the mistress herself came in to see if all was well. She went to the stove to taste the soup. She opened the oven to poke the roast. She peeked in the ice box to see the mousse. She waltzed to the pastry board to try a petit four. She picked a tiny lemon tart and was about to pop it in her mouth when she discerned with her keen eye an unsavory something on it. Indeed it was a dropping. She threw it in the air and shrieked. And this upset Violet so. He took frenzied flight and collided into a window. But again and again. And the mistress screeched, "Call the Sanitation Control! Call the Sanitation Control! Call the Sanitation Control!"

Cécile woke up. Her throat was very dry, and she blinked her eyes somewhat desperately. She heard the shrill voices of children around her and the shuffle of running feet. She was no longer in the dewy garden but in the public one, on a green park bench. She sat herself up and adjusted her hair pins. For a few minutes she sat there, dazed and disheveled. Then she got up and headed for the bus stop.

What she could not have known then, but which others may have noticed without caring to, was that on the back of the skirt of the blue suit, there was a stain. It was a blood stain. When she got back to her utility studio, she would undress and find it. And as rigorously and as unemotionally as a military nurse, she would scrub it clean. Perhaps several weeks later the thought of it might come back to her and she would weep. For the unfathomable and for the souls of those without souls.

My Temple, Oh Temple

Judith was a Christian. She was a modern Christian girl who had done chiropody studies at the Four Wings Christian College. She was an assiduous churchgoer and punctually attended the nine o'clock service, wearing periwinkle satin pumps to match her Sunday dresses, which she cinched in at the waist with a cream-colored cummerbund. She was always well groomed, trim, and wore her chestnut hair in an impeccable bob. Perhaps she was even pretty in a no-nonsense way.

It was her habit to stay after the church service for the coffee social to visit with the other Christians. And there everyone was the host or the hostess of the other, everyone there forgave the trespasses and smiled benevolently upon his neighbors. Judith was filled at these occasions with great love for her kind and whispered to herself with conviction, "They'll know we are Christians by our love, by our love. Yes, they'll know we are Christians by our love." Then she would bow her head and shake it gently; a gesture which plainly bespoke, Hallelujah!

One Sunday after a particularly moving sermon, Judith walked home from the Chowchilla First Presbyterian Church reading a pamphlet that had been handed to her by the Reverend Bob Hardman. If anyone had spotted her then he would have shouted a warning at her, "Careful there, Miss, watch your step!" for she was traipsing unsteadily across a fig orchard, her ankles buckling every fifth step or so. But she seemed to be hardly aware of this difficulty. She was much too absorbed in her reading to take notice. This is what she read:

I. The man who single-handedly brought Egypt to her knees, who wrote one-fourth of the Old Testament, who knew God intimately, and who gave us the Ten Commandments, was so depressed at one time that he said, "I want to die." His name was Moses.

II. The man who survived 72 hours in the belly of a whale at the bottom of the Mediterranean and then later preached to the world's most wicked nation, and saw 120,000 of earth's most evil heathens turn to God, was at one time so depressed that he said, "I want to die." His name was Johah.

III. The man who controlled Israel's weather by his prayers for seven years, who raised the dead, who rebuked his king, who called down fire from heaven, and who defeated 450 of the prophets of Baal, was at one time so depressed that he said, "I want to die."

Thirty-five million people battle depression in our country alone.

"Depression . . . ," said Judith, listening to her voice as if it were discovering the illness. "My God I'm depressed.

I'm absolutely depressed!" She reread the Reverend Mr. Hardman's text and went carefully over the words, measuring their sounds and losing their significations. These words Judith did not take to heart but to another vital place, perhaps to her soul. She weighed them in that crux below her chest and dropped heavily to her knees. There was nothing defiant about her at that moment. She did not wave her fist but wailed to the heavens, "The woman who took the Men of Nations to her bed, the Christian Armies, who tamed the beasts, and who kept her temple chaste all the while, was at one time so depressed that she said, 'I want to die!' Her name is Judith."

And with this Judith dropped her head down to the earth and pounded it there against the hard-pan soil as if she were knocking on the gates of the forefathers, those spiritual giants, to give her succor. For despite the reassuring words of the Reverend Mr. Hardman, she felt alone in her desolation. And perhaps her desolation was precisely that: loneliness. She had never been alone before but had always filled her rooms with gentlemen, and foot patients. What had happened of late? Her rooms were gaining in space and terror. Her sofas were losing weight and her armchairs (good God those armchairs!) were too slick, too shiny. Unbearable! Her home had become a blaring call and reminder of All That Is Forgotten. Yet it was good that she remembered she was forgotten. She was merely depressed. Things could have been worse. She might have forgotten entirely what had been forgotten. And where would she have been then? Worse off certainly.

But this was a new turn of events and up until then, Judith's life had been full and enjoyable and had allowed little time to sit and fret in orchards. She had her own practice as a chiropodist and was the reader at a weekly prayer meeting. Until she was thirty she had numerous lovers whose names she noted in a ledger, which she kept at her bedside table, beneath the Living Bible. She believed according to the Christian faith, that her body was her temple and so respected it and worshiped in it dutifully and attended to its need for pleasure and sensual encounters. She was what one might call a healthy, young woman, a woman who could delight herself in a variety of ways. She could try on a taboo to see how it fit. She discarded what burdened or embittered her and found new, lighter vestments and tastier viands. She was, to put it simply, a woman who took care of herself, this "herself" which was an inexact core frequented by others, a harbor of bodily and spiritual exchanges made in her name. Judith was attentive and made choices that appealed to her sense of joy and reason. She was not a hedonist however. Pleasure to her was good but not the chief good. Christ's bounty was the chief good. The temple and her lovers were good but not nearly as good as the Principle Good. She kept to reasonable proportions and to the laws. Yes, as a modern Christian girl, she had established her personal guidelines of dos and don'ts. These were what she called the Laws of the Temple. Judith read the newspapers and knew what was happening in the world. She had heard of the diseases spread so perversely from bed to bed with no thought of the morrow and could, if she were asked to, draw upon a blackboard diagrams explaining the precautionary measures to avoid these maladies. She was able then to lead each man, each gallant victor of her accord, carefully through that terra incognita, herself, so that he understood its byways and respected its regulations. To any refractory, stubborn man not yielding to treatment, she would say, "Step out of this blessed bed! Step! Step!"

The Laws of the Temple were in truth a recitation of sorts, a short declamation that Judith repeated by memory before each lover, new, old, or borrowed. It went something like this: "You may not enter the temple without a prophylactic. Above the temple door is the horseshoe of good fortune. Kiss it four times and your luck will be bettered. No pagan acts may be performed without consent. But ask and you shall receive." Judith did not believe in depriving herself or anyone else of a mutual delight but she was never heady or rash. She administered to the momentary desires all the while keeping sight of the hours apart and the days to come during which she would follow, separate from him, her peripatetics.

Judith accepted all the men she was with unconditionally and was more or less unconcerned with what she liked or disliked about them. When she was with Doudou Camara, the famous dancer of the tropics, she tended to his oversized feet without a comment. Whatever she may have thought of them she did not express. Perhaps she did not allow herself a fetish. Christian girls often didn't. She had no expectations and even if she were proposed to and given an engagement ring, as had indeed happened before, she would not have anticipated the ceremony plighting troths, she would not have entertained the idea of its possibility. It could be that she had never been in love. She had, however, loved each man she had been with, in a sincere and tidy way. As a result of this, men felt secure in their manhood when they were with her and rarely faltered or lost heart.

Although Judith could grow very close to a man, her greatest intimacy was, without question whatsoever, with Christ. When she knelt beside her bed in communion with Him, this was her most intimate gesture. "The Lord is my shepherd. I shall not want. . . ," she whispered to Him. And she did not want. She didn't ask for anything. She sought, but in a way that most would consider insufficient, for there was no passion in her seeking and only a meager spark of desire in it that was like the quick flame of a cigarette lighter.

Judith lived the first twenty-nine years of her life this way, as if bathed in the all-encompassing love and blessing of Christ. And while she would bleed for this singular love, for the numerous others she remained merely neat and intact. She clearly saw the difference between the two and did not confuse one for the other. She was content to live in this manner.

It was on Judith's thirtieth birthday that she met Heraldo, and on this occasion, she failed to differentiate the encounter from any of the previous ones she had had, as she had never before bothered to see the potential in a man. She made no exception for Heraldo at first and treated him kindly and coquettishly as she would any other. The night of her birthday, Judith went to a prayer meeting, after which a surprise birthday party in her honor had been organized. The members of the Christian Fellowship group had lovingly baked cakes and pastries for the occasion. They brought fruit juices too. It was also a tradi-

tion of theirs to invite outsiders to these worship celebra-
tions so that others too, could feel the love of their breth-
ren in Christ. Heraldo was one such guest. He was the
guest of the Reverend Mr. Hardman himself. Heraldo was
his doctor and a Catholic and had agreed to come not out
of curiosity but out of politeness, for the Reverend Mr.
Hardman had invited him time and again, and as he could
no longer politely refuse, he graciously accepted the offer.

Heraldo was a small, wiry Mexican of forty. He had an
ailing leg and a rather beautiful head. It was a head that
made one imagine him as a man of aristocratic birth who
perhaps had been reared as a foundling. There was mod-
esty and propriety to it and a fierceness too. His expressions were contradictory but splendidly so, and intriguing.
In his eyes one might devine an excess of a brooding,
almost unkind pride while the shape of his mouth revealed
a great longing, perhaps an inappropriate one, for it was
puzzling, and the extent of it could not quite be guessed.
His upper lip was adorned with a black mustache which
curled sensually, if not wickedly, as he spoke. He spoke to
everyone at the gathering and with such gregarious ease
that not a one badgered him with Christian convictions.
Heraldo was not a man to be badgered in any case.

Judith did not notice him that evening until the Happy
Birthday was sung. One voice rose above the others in
beauty and richness of timbre and when she looked up, for
her head was bowed with humility, she saw Heraldo before her and recognized him as the source of the voice she
was hearing. After the cake was cut and the toasts were
made, she went over to him and welcomed him to the
Christian Fellowship group.

"I heard you sing. You have a lovely voice," she said to him warmly. "We have a choir here, you know. And we're always looking for more singers. Would you be interested in joining us?"

"I don't think you would like my singing," he told her, smiling at her somewhat crookedly. "You see, I am a mariachi singer. I'm afraid I wouldn't know how to sing your gospel hymns."

"Oh well they're easy enough to learn," she went on. "Come over and I'll teach you some of them. I don't sing well but I can play the piano. You'll catch on quickly I can tell."

Heraldo accepted the invitation and this time not out of politeness, as with the Reverend Mr. Hardman, but out of curiosity. He wanted to know what this Christian girl was about to show him. While he thought he knew all about her kind, he realized that in truth he knew very little about the modern Christian girl. So he drove both of them to her apartment and parked where she suggested he park and walked up two flights of stairs to her landing. She invited him in and offered him some tea. Then as the kettle heated up, she got out her sheet music and sat down at the piano. She hiked her skirt up her thighs as if to manipulate the pedals she had to bare her legs. She also unbuttonned her blouse several buttons, to free her arms perhaps. Heraldo was a man and took mental note of this, saying mockingly to himself, "So this is what a modern Christian girl does when she teaches a man the gospel, she shows him her breasts and thighs." Judith was playing scales to warm up her fingers. "Come here and sit next to me so that you can read the words." she said to him, patting the piano bench.

Heraldo sat next to her and began playing. First he played an air in major, then one in minor, and before he could attempt whatever was to follow, Judith began kissing him fervently about the face. Her hands were on him, grabbing at him urgently. Then suddenly she stopped and began undressing herself, and as she pulled off her clothes, she recited the Laws of the Temple, as a Catholic might recite the rosary, by rote and seriously.

"You may not enter the temple without a prophylactic. Above the temple door is the horseshoe of good fortune. Kiss it four . . ."

"What?" Heraldo interrupted her. "What is this nonsense? Do you think that because I am a man you have asked to your home that I will sleep with you? Do you think that because I am a man I have no respect for your body, this temple that you call it, and that you must protect yourself from me? You do not know me then. I am Heraldo. I will take care of you, but you must let me do so. You are a man-fearing woman who trusts only in God. I never thought I'd meet one such as you. In my country women fear men and God and are victims of both. You think that you are saved, but you are not. You haven't yet learned to trust what is flesh, blood, and bone beneath and above you. But one day you will and you will say, My God, the fruit!"

Judith staggered back to the piano bench and sat down. Her shoulders slumped and her breasts sagged a bit between her arms. She sat like this for a moment and tried to think. She had never been spoken to in this way by a man before. In fact, she felt as if this were the first time she had heard a man speak to her. Hadn't she been listening before? Yes she had, but maybe only to the lilt of the phrases, the tremolo of a voice, and not to the words themselves. Here she heard the words and wondered what they could mean. Had he rejected her? No, she knew it wasn't quite this. He had, she felt, tapped her gently but firmly on the shoulder, as one might do to a distracted person so that he remembers his whereabouts. And Judith wanted to shout to him, "But if you knew what was out there, what your own kind was like, you would do the same!" But she did not. She sensed that he knew all there was to know about these things. He was saying very clearly that he was different; not in his desires but in how he undertook them. He was a man who likened his desire to a project to be attended to thoughtfully and with knowledgeable care. He did not sew his desires as the young man does his wild oats. He was, after all, a doctor of medicine and had been trained in methodology and in preventative health care.

Judith dressed herself slowly, as her mind sped through what she knew and was trying to know. She said to herself, "There are women and men and there is Christ who is the Son of Man." Then she wondered at this. She wondered at Man. She asked herself how Christ who was man was different from men and found this easy to explain. Christ was immaculately conceived; men were born in sin. Christ was a paragon of altruism, men were selfish. Christ was her protector, she needed protection from men. Who then was this man before her? This man claiming that he expected nothing from her but herself, her vulnerable self so that he could protect her? She finished buttoning her blouse and looked at Heraldo quizzically.

"Who are you?" she asked.

The man laughed hoarsely and looked at her with an intent in his gaze that she couldn't quite interpret. "I am Heraldo." He then walked over to the door, peered at her once over his shoulder and went out. It was like this that Judith, who had often wondered what it would be like to be left behind, was left behind.

When Judith awoke the following morning, she lifted her arms out to her sides and held them there for a moment, looking down at her chest. "Every woman is a cross," she muttered to herself. That day she called his office and made an appointment with his secretary to see him that week. She complained of a chronic backache. When she arrived at the office she was told to have a seat in the waiting room where there were four other people reading worn magazines. She waited ten minutes or so and was led by a nurse into a room where she was asked to undress and put on a white, onionskin robe. She did this and smoothed the crinkly tunic so that it rested against her body and didn't bellow out. She waited for the doctor, the Doctor Heraldo. There was a little round clock on the wall, and she watched it closely. At exactly five past the hour, he walked in without looking up, his head bowed over a clipboard he was holding.

"Hello," she said slowly.

Upon hearing her, Heraldo looked up to see his patient, one of many that day. A faint wave of surprise rushed across his face.

"Hello, Judith," he said in his doctor's voice. "What brings you here?"

"I've come here today because I'm ready and you know it. The last time I saw you I wasn't. But now I am ready."

"Yes, I see that you are. But what makes you think that I am ready?"

"You're ready because you're a man. Men are always ready."

Heraldo did not argue with her on this point but undid the robe which normally she would have undone and took off his medical clothes which she would have taken off had he let her. Every attempt she made to orchestrate the event was thwarted by Heraldo whose only words to her were "trust me." And so she loosened her grip and traced with her index finger the words, "I am not afraid of Heraldo," on her lover's back, over and over again, throughout their embrace until the last waves of pleasure came and subsided. This time she hadn't been greedy as she often was. She waited for the novelty, and it came as unexpectedly as a thief in the night.

As the months went by, Judith grew close to Heraldo and thought solely of him, of his attractive head and his sick leg, which she tenderly loved. She saw him exclusively and broke off her other dates. She attended Catholic weddings on the weekend to hear him sing, and Catholic funerals too. He took her to a Cinco de Mayo parade where she was blindfolded and spun. She was then handed a broom and told to hit the piñata. She did it too, in one grand slam. They loved her for it! Everyone scrambled to pick up the treats, and she, the winner, stood still above them all, wrapped in Heraldo's arms. She played other heathen games too, and once even posed as the Virgin Queen for the Procession of Our Lady of Guadalupe. Roses were thrown at her feet by the children. Thousands of them blanketed her lap. She reveled in these petals and said quietly, as she wasn't to speak, "I have enough love. I have enough love for you all!"

Yet her life was still solemn a good part of the time. She continued her chiropody practice and going to church and to Bible readings. Only there was less fervor in her approach to these activities. She didn't seem to find the same satisfaction in them as before. Perhaps she was less needy for these things. When the Reverend Mr. Hardman asked her to organize the Christian Fellowship annual potluck dinner, she told him that she didn't have the time. Nor did she feel any guilt in refusing him. Indeed she didn't have the time for such things. Her time had become Heraldo's time. And not through any sort of poor management on her part, but because of love. Wasn't that one of the greater gifts, the giving up of one's time? It is another way that one dies for another. "Christ died for me and you," Judith had often said to the others at the Bible readings. "Because of his love for us he died at the age of thirty-three." Judith was a student and believer of extremes. She had always kept her health because of her ability to balance between them; good and evil, deprivation and gluttony, pleasure and pain. She was able to stay on this middling ground because she had studied the nature of each excess. It was all in the Good Book. However since she met Heraldo, she discovered herself no longer in the middle but somewhere on a precipitous edge, leaning out dangerously. She was exhilarated. Heraldo cooked for her and made sumptuous dishes with mole sauces and Judith, who before had had little appetite, was ravenously hungry each time she sat down to a meal. She ate and ate and Heraldo would say to her, "Now you are looking more like a woman of my country. Now you are looking beautiful. Ah my love! It is a pleasure to watch you eat."

It was true that Judith was feeling herself to be more beautiful than ever. And with this beauty came a certain frivolousness, a lightness that was new to her. Perhaps she had escaped the puritan yoke, that weighty crosspiece on her soul that had made her judge too quickly and surely. It happened that she took the Lord's name in vain and felt like an accomplice in doing so. She laid her cards out on the table, too many of them and all at once. When Heraldo asked her the time, she took to answering him in mysterious ways. "Lover, it is time!" She lived, breathed, and ate with the man.

Heraldo and Judith remained lovers for six months and two days. On the eve of the third day after six months and two days of being together, Heraldo left Judith. He left her for another woman, who was his wife. It all happened too suddenly for Judith who was told over dinner; it was too soon and too impossible to digest.

"But where are you going?" she asked him as she held onto his hand.

"To Mexico to be with my wife and my children. To work with my people."

"You mean you're married? You never told me that! In all this time you never told me," said Judith appealing to him.

"Nor did you ask me."

Judith looked at him incredulously; not so much with disbelief in what he was saying, but with disbelief of the searing wound that was making its way across her chest.

"But what am I supposed to do with all this? With all

this?" She asked him as she pounded her fist against her heart, showing him the location of her pain.

"That's all you now, Judith. It's you. It's what you are and what you have."

Heraldo left Judith like this, as swiftly as he had the day she had tried to ravish him at the piano. He glanced at her quickly over his shoulder and stepped out the door. For days Judith had a low-grade numbness in her heart. It throbbed as all wounded things do, silently and contagiously. People felt sad around her and avoided her, even the Christians. She went about her doings as usual although she did them without pleasure. It was only a lingering sense of duty that kept her examining feet and reading the gospel.

The Saturday night before the Sunday that the Reverend Bob Hardman made his moving sermon that sent her walking across the fig orchard in a great reverie, Judith had a series of erotic dreams, dreams in which the men she had known appeared, those that were part of what she called the Christian Army. In dream tongue they called her the Temple of Galilee, the Woman of Wants, and worshiped her in the most carnal of fashions. When Judith awoke she was weeping. She wept herself into convulsions and vomited the little she had eaten the night before. She was miserable and this purging did nothing to assuage the sickened condition of her heart, her erotic muscle. When this moment of violence had passed, she was as she had been before, with a dull, throbbing chest, a pain that was so familiar, it had become a habit, something to be taken for granted.

On her knees in the fig orchard, Judith recognized the

name of her habit, it was depression. It became to her then, a thing to observe and to hold in the hand. Just the thought of the word made her rock on her calves and hold her body tightly with crossed arms. She rocked for some time, moaning until she felt something hit her head. This startled her, and she stood up brusquely, touching her head to feel what had landed on her. It was a fig. A fat, overripe, purple fig that would burden the tree no longer. It was sticky and pulpy in Judith's hair and in her hand as she cupped it. "The sky is falling," she said to herself. And she laughed. She laughed wildly, with as much abandon as she had cried that morning. It was the laugh of the last Christian girl.

The Builder

*I*n Egypt, Naima and Samir Beyoumi bore many daughters, then finally a son, Sliman, who came into the world with a clubfoot. This foot kept his peace in the world as sometimes arms will do for nations; indeed, it could be said he was armed at the foot. Sliman worked as a cameraman in the city of Cairo and owned a small home with a terrace. His services were demanded quite regularly and he did this job well despite his clubfoot. In fact the clubfoot was hardly a hindrance to his professional life in Egypt as he could keep pace with others when walking and even run on occasion, not clumsily, but with the unexpected grace of that which is syncopated. His feet accented the ground a bit differently than most, but this was not a problem in itself, it was simply a novel rhythm to make acquaintance with and then to leave alone. Those who knew the man well thought nothing of it. When they heard the displaced beat approach, they thought, "Ah! there is Sliman," and not "Ah! I hear the clubfoot!" In Cairo, where he lived and worked and made merry, Sliman had been regarded as nothing more and nothing less than a whole man. This held true except upon one occasion, which was the draft day of his eighteenth year. He received a notice of exemption from the service on account of physical deformity; he was considered not to have the makings, the manly stuff, of a soldier of Egypt. And although this wounded his pride, he did not take it so sorely, for in fact, because of this dismissal, he managed to find another door, that of the Technical School of Audio Visual Trades, which opened itself to him with the small scholarship he had procured. And so he happened upon the métier of cameraman, perhaps one could say, because of his foot, this hoof that shortly after accouchement, had kicked his mother sharply in the jaw and made her weep. But only because she loved him so.

Sliman was quite a small man, a little over five feet in height and also very slender. His head was little more than a skull and his black, strawlike hair adhered flatly to it. He had prominent but scarred cheekbones and dark sunken eyes that even in his adult life retained the sweetness and candor of the Sem Sem bird. He would, perhaps, have passed through the cafés and streets of Cairo largely unnoticed had he not had these appealing eyes that no honest man or woman could ignore in clear conscience. Indeed he was pleading but neither for things nor attentions, rather he begged the acceptance of his particular nature, which he himself, until the age of twenty-two, accepted only with great difficulty. His nature was much of a mystery until then, a hint of malaise in his blood. He could only sense its ache and for this it was a burden.

It was at twenty-two, that this nature was revealed to him. Sliman, in those early days of his manhood, experienced an event, a chimerical revelation from which he could not wake entirely but with which he could not sleep soundly. He was shown his nature in a singular dream, and it preoccupied him completely, heart, soul, and member. This was the dream: He was sitting on the banks of the Nile, his legs outstretched in front of him, when a dervish approached him twirling and uttering the words, "Khepi rejlek yakhouya bismi'llah (Hide that foot, brother, in the name of Allah!)." Sliman was so taken back and ashamed at this pronouncement, that he began fervently to bury his clubfoot in the sand. However, when it was entirely covered and the sand was hard packed about it, his hands didn't stop but continued on, constructing castles, not the those of Arabia, but castles of a northern land, the castles of France. These were the ones he was building, yet as his hands mounded and shaped the sand, it slowly took on another consistency, a stiffer yet more tenacious one. Through some alchemical process, the sand had become his own flesh, and he was molding his own foot. His foot had been taken and then given back to him in a form of matter that he could mold and nourish into something of beauty. Indeed, his blood was rising through the veins of the walls, the turrets, the subterranean passages, and the dungeons. And the castles came to life and were sustained by the life blood of a life's foot.

When Sliman awoke from this dream, he felt with certainty that he had been handed the map of his destiny, his *mektoub,* according to the will of Allah. It was the dream that blessed his past, wept for his present, and gave horizon to his future. "Yes," he solemnly acknowledged to himself upon waking, "from my foot I have built castles. From my hands I will build palaces. I am a cameraman by trade but a builder by nature." Then to his God he added, "Allah, may I be true to your will, which is the seed you have planted in me!"

Now, this was not so much what Sliman understood of his nature but how he interpreted it. He kept in mind the formalities, the presentation, but did not search beneath them. He had no notion that one might separate inner from outer truths, distinguish truth from metaphor. He began, then, to plan his journey to Paris, France.

When his family heard of this, they were at first bewildered by the idea, then alarmed by it. And when Sliman sold his house with a terrace to buy his plane ticket, they were utterly distressed, for this made it clear to them that the departure was imminent.

"Why Sliman," his mother would ask, "do you sell your home to go where you won't have one? There is nothing for you there. You will forget Ramadan and eat at noontime. Ill fortune comes from this. And the women, my son. They are not for you. They have sweet tongues but smell foul and expensive. At least marry an Egyptian girl before you go to take with you. She can help you in many ways."

"Perhaps you are right. I will find a wife before I go. But don't worry. When you know what Allah has said, you know what you must do. And I know. One day you will hear of me the way you hear of a potentate, someone great and distant."

It was doubtful that Sliman believed all he told his mother for he was essentially a humble man. Yet he wanted his mother to be proud of him and not tormented or shamed by his doings. He himself, felt none of these emotions. He seemed to walk in a dark cloak of certainty which hid all peripheries from his view. What he did see was sound and sure, irrefutable. Some would call such certitude bliss. At the heart of it was a blind spot, a love of abandon. In a word, it was faith, assembled for him by the hands of his Maker. He had only to step along the path, even the rhythm of his feet, the offbeat was accounted for.

It so happened then, that without seeking a wife, Sliman found one. His sisters took the matter in their own hands and presented him the little Affifa, whom they found behind a sack of dried peppers at the market place one morning. At first she would not come with them and held obstinately to the burlap sack of peppers.

"Why should I go and marry him? What's he got?" she asked.

"He has sold his house and now he's looking for a wife. He's going to France to build."

There was a moment of silence before Affifa responded, although the decision had been made instantly upon the mention of France.

"OK then," she said in a cool voice which her eyes, suddenly cunning and sharp, nearly betrayed. "I'll have a look." She followed the sisters then, to the family home.

Affifa was seventeen and so tiny that she could have

been considered a midget. Indeed perhaps she was one. Otherwise she was perfectly made, with such delicacy of bone and skin that one dared not touch her for fear of bruising her. She had long, jet-black hair and a shiny face, which she conditioned with virgin olive oils. At times she surreptitiously made punctual, rodentlike movements toward her forehead, breast, and shoulders with her right hand. She was, in fact, making the sign of the cross but no one recognized it as this. Perhaps they thought she was playing a game that she had been taught at the orphanage school, for the only thing that was known about Affifa was that she was an orphan. And for this the Beyoumi family loved her all the more and took her under their wing more tenderly than they would have another. What they did not know about this orphanage was that it was tended by Roman Catholic sisters from France, the Soeurs de la Conception Immaculée. Nor would they ever have guessed this as, when with them, the young girl adhered to Muslim customs so convincingly. Had they known, Affifa realized, that she was a Catholic, they would not have agreed to the marriage and her trip to France would have been subsequently lost. And this chance she simply could not afford to lose, for more than anything in the world, the orphan girl desired to go to France, to that country where the Virgin Mary made numerous apparitions and left holy shrines in her wake. She saw herself bathing in the waters of Lourdes, in the waters of the only mother she had ever known, the Blessed Mother. And such great love would come from this! She had heard the stories from the sisters, knew them by heart, and wanted to make her pilgrimage to the Holy Mother's sites, to reach her grail this way.

The month that she spent with the Beyoumis, in preparation for the nuptials and voyage, she kept all this hidden and took to the ways of Sliman's sisters with extraordinary savoir faire. She hennaed her hair and let her fingers keep the stain according to custom. All were charmed by and pleased with her, especially Sliman, who twice wept at her feet, at the thought of possessing her in wedlock. She was piquant and stirred in him tremendous appetence for pleasing.

"You will see, Affifa. In France I will build you a castle with chairs your size so that your pretty feet will touch and bless the ground where you sit," Sliman would say to her.

"Ah yes, you will do that," she would reply, nodding her head compliantly, fluttering her eyelashes toward the floor. She played coy and feigned loyalty and faith in Man. Sliman was enchanted.

It was upon the very wedding day, in the evening after all the ceremony, that the newlyweds boarded the plane to Paris. Sliman carried a suitcase and Affifa two, which she had made so heavy that they were fined a tax. This dismayed Sliman for he had, in fact, so little money, despite having sold his house with a terrace. Most of that money went for the plane fare and what was left would have to be carefully managed. However, as he did not feel right telling his delicate bride whose love for him had not yet been consummated, to leave her chattels behind her, he paid the fee without a word. So it was that the honeymooners spent their first night together in economy class en route to Paris. And although a certain fear of the unknown should perhaps have bound them in solidarity, neither had any apprehension, for they both had anticipated this trip. However, they had not anticipated it in detail, because if they had, they might have been put off by the complications, but as a navigable and necessary point on the chart. Both confused anticipation with knowing. One anticipated his vocation, the other the realization of her desire. But neither knew in any exact way where these impulses would lead them.

When the couple did reach Paris, they made their way to Sliman's cousin Elie's place. Elie lived in an immigrants' hotel for men on the rue Crimée. It was a dilapidated building a block long with half-boarded windows out of which hung washing, blue worker's overalls, random socks, and an occasional brassiere. Although the men were not allowed to house women, many managed to live there with their wives for it merely took a bottle of pastis to cajole the concierge into letting them lead a woman up the stairs. And usually, once a woman found her way to the upper floors, she didn't come down much, but nested above. It was a place where a homeless woman could find pleasure and some ease.

Elie, as it turned out, roomed with a Polish ex-priest named Wronski on the third floor with a window facing courtyard side. Each man had a single bed, Elie's on the right, Wronski's on the left. The right side of the room was sparsely decorated with ornamental poufs and potteries. The left wall, however, was cluttered with religious bric-a-brac, a hoard of ecclesiastic memorabilia. There was something at once desperate and clownish about this wall, as if a secular but frantic hand had disguised it as religious. Perhaps the hand of a man who on bad days, lay himself down cruciform, questioning, "If I believe in miracles, must I believe in God?" This was Wronski, a small, white-haired fellow with wire glasses who smacked his lips too often and was witness time and again to miracles. He was rarely taken seriously, this Wronski, but perhaps this was because of the patois he spoke. Nobody understood it. He often flailed his arms and giggled, "Ah oui, oui, oui", or "Ah non, non, non."

When the couple arrived with their luggage and he saw that they would be staying, he affected an officious gallantry and offered his bed to the fatigued Affifa.

"Madame," he said to her pushing his index finger into the bed, "This for you. Here for you. Oui, oui, oui."

Affifa noticed his face reddening and sat down on the mattress before he colored more. It was both his anxiety to be understood and the presence of this tiny but lovely girl that made him blush so.

"Thank you, father. That's kind of you," Affifa reassured him, stroking him with her eyes.

"Ah! My little one! My little one! Oui, oui, oui!" muttered Wronski, fluttering his arms and leaving the room, like a cuckoo bird having heralded the hour.

Wronski had genuinely given up his bed to the bride for, from that night on he no longer slept in his room although he did come back every morning and spent his days there. It was not known where he slept but in the mornings he nearly spooked the others with his crisp alacrity, his gregarious homilies. He was fresh and well reposed and his hair stood on end.

On their second day in Paris, Elie took Sliman to his foreman, Raoul, to try to get him work.

"This is hard work, Sliman. Nobody likes it. But there's a hot meal at noon and the other men aren't so bad." Elie said to him as they approached the construction site.

"Oh," said Sliman, "But this is why I came. I came to build you see. First I will start here, with this building. It's a nice one and will house many families. But one day I will build a magnificent ornament that will exist only because it is beautiful. It will hold no one but invite all to behold its beauty."

"Ah! Now that would take big money. You got any of that, Cousin?" mocked Elie.

"No, but you will see, Elie. It does not take so much money, really. Because it is Allah who wants it so. I know it is within my means." The two cousins said no more to each other but continued up the street to the trailer which served as Raoul's office. When they entered, Raoul, a bulky man with a thick, square jaw, was bellowing at a wispy African man in a red ski bonnet, who, they gathered from the gripe, was a cement mixer. When this man slithered away, Elie stepped up to the desk with Sliman to his right.

"Hello, Boss, this is my cousin Sliman. He's looking for some work at the site."

Raoul being a very astute man had noticed the clubfoot even though hotly engaged with the cement mixer.

"Don't take any handicaps here. Never get the work done that way."

"Who's handicapped?" piped up Sliman. "I am a builder like him, my cousin. That's why I'm here!"

"Sorry. I can't take him," said the contractor, still addressing Elie. "We've got deadlines to meet here."

It was only after some effort that Elie managed to get Sliman work as a painter at another construction site which was further along. Sliman watched the other men with a sigh that sunk to his bowels. He watched them handling saws and drills, hammers and picks. He saw the nails and the lathes, the bulldozers and the sledgehammers, all of these put to work, making a muscular din. He heard the harmony of toil and tool and echoed this music in his own ear so that it was his. Yet all the while he held in his hand a paintbrush which day after day he pushed up and down walls, here and there. In dwellings and offices to be. He held it, but unconvincingly. It had a music too, but like that of a moaning and prolonged organ note. Sliman found himself apprentice to a new trade, one so vacuous it was learned by rote. Everyday he asked for carpentry work at the site and everyday he was turned away and handed a paint can. But Sliman had great wells of patience and continued on. He needed the money badly, as he did want to take an apartment for himself and his wife. He found the immigrants' hotel for men hardly suitable for a newly wedded couple.

Indeed, the sleeping arrangements at the hotel rarely varied and displeased Sliman immensely; Elie slept in the bed on the right, Affifa in Wronski's bed, and Sliman assembled a sort of bedding for himself on the floor between the two. This is how they slept, except for the nights that Elie did not come home, which, in fact, weren't many.

This being the case, Sliman was more often than not, deprived of his conjugality. Several times he climbed into Wronski's bed to take comfort in his wife's arms, only to find himself with horror the next morning lying beside a battered, black and blue girl. How she bruised, as if her blood just waited for the slightest prompting to suck upon her skin. What he intended as caresses were blows. Ah! What was he to build with this woman? Neither love nor family. He had married an untouchable girl.

If Sliman disliked hurting his wife, which indeed he did very much, Affifa was simply peeved by it. In general she did not care to be touched or physically coddled by him. And she did not submit to her husband without voicing her dismay.

"Ah husband! Hurry up then. Let it be done with and leave me in peace!" she would say as Sliman groped above her. Her voice was sharp and wrought in him a feeling of self-loathing so acute that his manhood would at times fail him.

Affifa not only claimed Wronski's bed as her own, but the entire room as well. It became her domain, where she spent her days while the men worked. Wronski occupied it with her, although as a knight, her *serviteur*. She often sat around on the poufs playing little games with Wronski's deck of saint cards. Perhaps these were concentration games. Sometimes she would invite Wronski to join her, and he agreed to play, although he never understood the game nor its rules, for which the girl would reprimand him sternly. He always lost.

"Here, Wronski. These are for you. Hide them well."

"Oui, oui, oui."

"Not like that, Wronski! I see everything!"

"Oui, oui, oui."

"There, that's better. Let's go on . . ."

And she would set down a card of Saint Francis and beside it another of Saint Barbara. Then she would fold her arms and wait with defiant expectation for the ex-priest who was sweating and smacking his lips with desperation, to make his move. Of course when he did play his card, it was the wrong one, a Saint Angelo or a Saint Fiona.

"Ah no Wronski! You don't get it at all!" she would chastise him. Then she would go into his hand to pick out a card she could play to her advantage.

Wronski took part in any activity to which Affifa invited him. To her he spoke his three-ply affirmation, "oui, oui, oui," three words fastened under the tongue, then sent out to her in puckers. Indeed, it came to be the announcement of all she could have. She had only to glance at an object and he, reading her gaze, would tremble with excitement and offer it to her. "It's for madam! Oui, oui, oui!" What she particularly liked were his picture hagiologies. They were written in Polish but the drawings were lovely and she knew the stories in any case. She knew all about them. She would tell them aloud.

"Saint Bernadette," she once told him, "was so poor she had no undergarments. But when a sick man came to her, she was fearless. Even if a sick dog came. She had no fear. She dug her tongue deep into the wounds of man and beast and cured them this way. When the Virgin Mary came to her at the grotto, she said, 'I know you love mankind for your worth and the worth of gold. So do stop licking those sores. Tell the ill and the lame to bathe in these waters. I will heal them.' And so the diseased came and were cured in the spring. But then great mistrust, spurred by the powerful diocesan, swept the surrounding villages, and the girl Bernadette, was taken and fettered and made to wear a sorcerer's talisman at her breast. But evil could not withstand her for long, and the talisman which was an image of a Byzantine devil, began to shed tears of remorse. When the guards witnessed this, they too wept catharticly. Several rested their cheeks against her wet bosom to feel the miracle. When this was over, Bernadette was sopping wet but free of the shackles. She went back to the grotto, where the Virgin appeared to her with magnificent luminosity. 'My daughter,' she said, 'you have suffered, and the suffering have stopped coming to me. I hope you are feeling better. Tell them to go to the spring yonder and drink and wash themselves. Tell them the Son of man is at hand.' With this Bernadette went into ecstasy. The ecstasy lasted forty-five minutes. Then she took a bath. Soon many were going to the spring to be purified and cured. Bernadette was sent away to a distant convent where for the rest of her life she ate bitter herbs, drank muddy water, and was tortured by a nun named Carmela."

Having finished this story the Egyptian girl, bowed her head to allow for five seconds of silence. When she raised it, Wronski was before her, a man transfixed with his jaw hanging low and his tongue lying flaccid in its pool of saliva. He resembled a mad dog and when he lunged at her skirts, she almost jumped up with terror, but as she saw he was weeping, she instead let him nestle his head in her lap.

"Ah, my dear man," she said caressing his white head, "I see you are devoted to her. You love her too."

"Oui, oui, oui" uttered the ex-priest in a muffled and almost inaudible voice. "Oui, oui, oui."

"I am an orphan girl but I am not without a mother. She is the Blessed Mother of all."

"Oui, oui oui," gasped Wronski. He was inhaling her skirt with his sobs. It was a silk skirt and he had much of it in his mouth.

"Ba'ahebek ketir alachene bet'hebeha!" (It's your love for her that I love!)," she said in her own tongue.

And with this not another word was spoken, but in the room below a thud was heard, then a series of thumps, and finally a silence so perfect it was transparent to the ear. It was on this day that Affifa became an ex-priest's concubine and Sliman a cuckold.

Sliman did not take the time to worry about his wife's doings while he was at work, painting. He maintained a fundamental and unfounded trust in the woman and was besides much too preoccupied with the daily promulgation of his destiny by foremen and builders. He was promoted to the finer painting jobs and considered this a misfortune as he saw it as anchoring him more firmly in this trade at the expense of the truer one. But it was an undeniable fact that Sliman painted with a rare expertise. He tended to a wall so well. He could make a rough, discordant one smooth as a pane of colored glass. He had an infallible eye for color too, and was often called to mix the tints. Indeed, there was even a noted interior decorator, Jack Lalangue, who conferred with him on color schemes. Sliman could get the paint to match a color swatch perfectly. From this talent he did procure pleasure, although he refused to delight in it. "Delight," he told Elie once, "can only be felt when you are doing what you are meant to do. So you see, I have no delight. And Allah has no delight in me."

"But you are well paid and well esteemed. And you have a beautiful little wife. Surely you delight in that!"

"I'm afraid not. Lying on her is like lying on a banana. How she bruises!"

"Then you must learn to peel and eat her quickly," said the cousin with a mischievous smile.

Sliman said nothing more but was wounded by this remark and shamed too, for his cousin had guessed how things were between him and his wife in the two-bed room, and was offering advice. He found council of this sort intolerable for it made play of and cast doubt upon his manhood. Sliman was filled with a sentiment of worthlessness and promised himself in the harshest terms he knew, to become a builder soon, as this, he was certain would restore his wife's love and devotion to him. "She is ashamed of me," he thought to himself, "I must show her that I am what I am meant to be. Then she will be like other happy wives. She will be happy to please."

Sliman had grown somewhat shy of Affifa and did not look at her as he spoke to her. He did, nevertheless, notice that her face and arms were looking rather discolored and sore. He said nothing, however, not wanting to call attention to this in front of Elie. But it upset him deeply. Then, when it came time for Ramadan, it was clear that she had no intention of respecting the custom of fasting. Indeed she seemed oblivious of Ramadan. In the morning she would eat copiously, the sweet breads and cakes Wronski brought in with him, while the two Egyptian men abstained and went through their ritual *al salate,* or prayer.

It was not Sliman but Elie who questioned the girl.

"Has she forgotten it's Ramadan?" he asked her, speaking to her in the third person as he always did.

"Ha! Do I care!?" answered Affifa, her mouth full of doughnut.

"It doesn't concern her to be a good Muslim then."

"No, it doesn't."

This avowal so horrified Sliman, that he pretended not to hear it. He would not fathom it. It was impossible that he could have married such a woman. No, his wife was a devout Muslim girl. And if she was eating before sunset and behaving strangely Sliman thought, it could only be because she was with child. "Yes," said the man to himself, "She is a timid girl and has not told me, but now she has told me in so many words! We are blessed with a child!" This was his new certainty, his new affirmation in life and in his God. He felt himself glow with the warmth of this event. He felt debonair even. He put on a tie and wore it for ten days. But then he took it off on the eleventh, for it was on this day that he discovered that Affifa had left him. She had written a note and put it on Wronski's bed.

Dear first Husband,

I am going with the ex-priest Wronski on pilgrimage. We shall be very long I think. We may even go to Medjugorje. There is a special bus that takes pilgrims there. Maybe we will see each other again but if we don't, please do take another wife. As for me, I have a new husband. It's ex-priest Wronski.

When Sliman finished reading this note, he lay down on the bed which had been Wronski's and felt all the symptoms drain from him, out his jittering foot; the symptoms of his phantom pregnancies, the swelling of false delight, of love of woman, of renewal. He lay there until all the tissues and corpuscles of hope fled from him. This took an entire day during which he was aware only of the sensation and flux of loss. He awoke from this early in the morning hours and got up to relieve himself. However, he did not stand up on the feet he knew. The one foot, the clubfoot, which had kept his peace in the world, now twitched. It jerked almost incessantly so that he tripped and nearly fell several times on his way to the toilet.

In the morning, as Sliman could find nothing to do with himself or his sorrow, he went to work. He was put on a new assignment that day which was to paint out a wall in a city park which had been covered with lewd graffiti. This wall took him three days to paint white, a bit longer than it normally would have, as he was unsteady on his feet and when he finished late in the afternoon, he did not leave immediately after as he usually did, but for some reason unknown to him, sat down on a bench facing the wall and said a prayer.

"Allah, I have done a day's work and now before me is a wall. I can see it but not around it nor beyond it. Everyday it is this way." Then he raised his head as if delivering himself of a weight, and looking out, saw not a wall in front of him but a luminous and wavering presence, a stark but graceful apparition. He gazed at it transfixedly until its intensity of heat and light, increasing by the minute, forced him to look away. "Allah! What is it that you want? Tell me and I will do it!" But as he uttered these words, he understood what must be done.

Night had begun to fall in the park and the park guards were blowing their whistles for the strollers to leave. Sliman quickly hid his paints and ladder in the shrubbery and himself as well. Then he waited. He waited for the guards to leave and lock the gates so he could inherit the park. But this was not a calculative wait, during which he mapped out his project in his mind or on paper. The map was already in him, burning through his blood. The man had swallowed the phoenix. Soon it would be time to let the bird out.

When the last security car pulled out of the park and the heavy, wrought iron gate was locked behind it, Sliman got up from where he was sitting in the bushes and feverishly walked toward the wall with his paints. The wall was still as brilliant as before, only his eyes now, could stand the blinding glare. They were no longer afraid. They saw what the wall was meant to be. Sliman set his paints and brushes at the middle of the wall and began. With furious strokes of the brush he painted, yet it was as if the paint were already there, as if the image imprinted itself beneath the brush. All had been waiting for him, he had only to touch it with his hands and instruments and it would come into sight. He worked fast, standing like a flamingo on one foot. The clubfoot, which twitched fiercely, he held under his rump. And he forgot about it. He forgot his body as it painted his soul. He worked unknowingly with both hands and swept the paint across the wall in every direction at once, and yet with a formidable precision and attention to line and color. For four hours he painted in this way and covered the bottom half of the wall. And what he had built was the bottom half of a kingdom, the bottom half of the immigrants' hotel, redeemed, and its neighboring ornaments. He then climbed on his ladder and continued. The ladder was an excessively tall one, about two and a half times longer than the average home ladder. It was a painter's ladder. He started half way up it and continued his fresco there with the same force and velocity. And all through the night he moved his way up his ladder, up his kingdom. He met with his wife there. She was dressed in a shimmering silver gown and wore a garland of stars on her head. And he came face to face with himself, as a man who beheld all things. A man with a marble eye and a golden foot. A man with a hammer in his hand. In the early morning hours he reached the skyline to which he would give color, a peacock blue. But by this time the fire in his blood had cooled down not a little, and while he continued with the same expertise, he lacked the flourish and heady speed of the previous hours. He kept on but now with a sigh or two and a heaviness of limb. Then he finally reached the last section of the sky and realized after a moment of making a great effort at leaning out, that he ought to go down the ladder and move it to the left. But somehow the courage failed him to do this and instead, to get a better reach, he stood entirely on his left foot, that is to say the clubfoot, and leaned as far as possible toward the area to be painted. This worked. He was able to get to the spot. He painted with careful, deliberate strokes, knowing that they were the last ones and should be as perfect as the rest. He was leaning out quite a bit, on his toes in fact, and everything would have been fine had the foot not suddenly jumped. But it did, unexpectedly, like the Mexican jumping bean, and Sliman stood for a moment suspended in the air, the paint can still in his hand, before he fell. His fall was like that of many men before him, there was nothing to break it but the earth. Then all was silent in the park except for the occasional moans of lovers and muggers in the brush and the rustling of a man slowly gathering his limbs. There the mural stood, in the delicate morning light, a universe disguised as a jewel. There were no doors to enter it; the viewer's eye was its threshold.

The Mission San Martin

Christmas

Brothers and Sisters,

This year as with the years beforehand, I, the Père LeFève, write you from the Mission San Martin to wish you the joyous season greetings. For rejoice! The Lord hath come upon a Virgin! Hallelujah! The King of Kings is here. Not so? Brother and Sisters, you know the San Martin Mission because for many years I speak to you about its existence. But perhaps you don't know that many ignore completely this mission. This is the reason why it suffers so a loss of public and the monies that come from these giving persons. As the Father Junipero Serra who founded this one and many other ones in the eighteenth century, I do my best to spread the word. And the word is this: the Mission of San Martin is yet in life and needs your help to keep up! The Father Serra loved all his missions as his childrens. He conceived of these with great travail and inspired vocation. All so legitimate, all so lovely. In the eyes of God and Man. Why then is this one child, a beauty and peaceful place indeed, being treated as if it is the love child, the bastard, the fault of Joseph? This, my brothers and sisters is unjust. This thought must not be sanctified. God the Father does not make error. If the Mission San Martin exists, it exists for reasons. You make some efforts, I know, to contribute to the collections box. That the good Lord bless you and look upon you with misericorde. But, friends, this is never enough. You must keep it up and speak around you. Others will know and give. But it is up to you. It is your turn to give and to seek giveness. Please do.

As you are possibly awares, I bumped into my ex-parish in Madera, California, for a fine surprise. This was in October and many of you, Brothers and Sisters, I did see there. You were all in such fine shapes, I hope that this is true even in this moment that I write you. How to tell you what pleasure to find you there!? Really unbelievable, my friends! "Père LeFève," many of you supplicated, "Please come again. We wait with impatience for you." Ah, my friends. It is necessary that I leave. But I will come again. You know of my fidelity to the Mission San Martin and must respect this. I was called from my motherland, the France, to occupy myself with it. I left delights of culinary preparation so delicious and wonderful, foods you, habitants of this land, cannot know because they have no existence here, to consecrate myself to this mission and to the good works. Such sacrifices are rare these, our days. But I made them. Now, I reap.

Brother and Sisters, the intention of this letter is all the more urgent that I just discovered, two days ago, that a robber come and gone. It was the mission safe which he arrived at opening without sounds to warn us. The sums that he took? Some four thousand dollars. This is to say, all we had! Unfortunately, as we all know, the Lord cannot reimburse us directly the money. He must do this through me and you. Mostly through you, given that I swear poverty, as you must realize. So it is that I and the Mission San Martin depend of you. Please pull in for us. Again, we are obliged to supplicate you.

We of course ask ourselves who is the culpable. Some fingers are pointing to the son of Señora Cruz, she who is the laundress. It is true that this boy is often about. He hangs what his mother washes. When he finishes his job he practices show-business. Show-business is this thing so much of the native boys do. They are show-bizzies. This is to say, they wear trouser and hats and vest that are quite magnificent, and make them stronger in beauty than their mothers. Many colors and agréments too. Very shocking boys. But silly and stupid! Lamentable childrens. They learn nothing and practice this show-business before the young girls. They are pretentious coqs! Hot rabbits! With fire in their fannies! If they work it is just to make better show-business, to have the possibility to buy more beauty habits and products for the hairs. It is rare that they give some money to the mothers who are always in difficulties. It is never! They think they must have this money and more to keep up show-business. I tell you, we suspect strongly that some of these boys do the thief to keep up. And for this reason we also suspect the son of Señora Cruz to rob. This is an understandable conclusion although we have no proofs. Ah! But it is difficult to learn such boys. Not so? They prefer show-business to good works.

Please my brothers and sisters, respond to me as soon as quickly. Remember that the good Lord gives to the giving. But he does not spare those who are spare. Not so? Best wishes to all of you who are still alive. And if you're yet alive, please give.

Merry X-mas and pray for me,
Père LeFève.

· · ·

Lent

Brother and Sisters,

Hello from the Mission San Martin in this season of Lent. As we know, Lent is a moment of abstinence so that the giveness is better. Jesus was in the desert for forty days and look what he gives us. Everlasting life! Not so? I ask you in a first time, to think of the daily costs of the meats you usually take for dinner. Multiply this by forty. Do you have the answer? In a second time, I ask you to do a check for this sum of the meats of which you abstain. This check you can send to the Mission San Martin, in care of me, the Père LeFève. I invite you to share the spirit. Remember the temptations of the desert, these temptations of indulgence, power and lust. Then remember that all such ones shall be overcome in the name of finer giveness. Give! Please do!

My brother and sisters, I must thank you for your generous help during the X-mas season. I appreciate that many between you made some efforts to make that season a cherry one. It was more cherry than we hoped. You heard our embarrassing circumstances, that is to say, the theft, and replied sooner than possible. Many thanks. However I hold to tell you that amongst your checks, were several which were without provisionment. So this provoked some contentions at the Banco Populario. And the result? The money doesn't come and the Mission San Martin in care of me, the Père LeFève, pay the price of this unfortunate story. I realize that you have some good intentions, but it is quite unfortunate that I must pay for your unsuccessful attempts at giveness. Please take care to escape such catastrophes in the future times.

So it is true that many have given but as I must always say, this is never enough. You must keep it up. If this letter reaches you when you are still alive, it is to tell you those three important words: Keep it up! In truth one must give up to keep up. Not so? For example, although you do not know, I gave up beloved things when I quit the France. The life is so different there. In the France, my friends, I am born in la Clinique de la Madeleine, that is to say, I translate for you, the Clinic of the Madeleine, on the rue St. Pierre le Gros Cailloux, the street of St. Peter the Fat Pebble. If only you know what delightful country this is. But you do not. It is true that one day, I will return to the patrie for my retreat. But of course, this is for when I will be old and out-dated. In a time to come. For the moment I am quite fine, digest well and guard my waist line. All these years, which really aren't so much, I keep all my hairs. As you know, I keep a good shape. Ah! If only you know the splendors of la France! They are so many to count! Such delight in the comestibles! How one eats well! Delicacies of the vine and all good fruits of the earth! They give water to the mouth. So many plates for the palate; mustard rabbit, tartares, orange duck, fat liver spread, fishes in truffle cream, thousand leaf pastry. You ignore completely these culinary refinements. Such a pity.

In the France, one eats well and one cannot regret at the death because of this goodness. There is no remorse in such bellies and so the death is peaceful. My dear sister, Marie-Laure, who lived her life in all devotion to the mystery of blood and flesh, in the Couvent de Notre Dame de la Mont Jolie, I translate, the Our Lady of the Pretty Mount Convent, is so perfectly an example of this. Her last words on her death bed were, "I have dined well this evening." That eve, the angel of death took her but did not take the after-dinner smile which framed her teeths. She died with much pleasure in her stomach. There is no better way to be deceased, my friends. I, who work on the sides of the life and the death, have many interviews with these that you call, undertakers. Believe me! That often they mention me the lamentable state of the entrails in their clients. "Ah" said a certain one, "warn your parishioners to eat better. Their bowels are black with poisons and so difficult to tidy." If the Catholic church, Holy and Roman, will survive this continent, its members must take care to survey their dining. As it is said here, "You are what you eat." Not so?

Brothers and Sisters, you must not believe that I preach you gluttony. No, it is not this. What I want to say is: All is in the Preparation! The Preparation is all! In this way, one can satisfy oneself with one sliver of ham if this meat is succulent from being hacked with a cleaver from the hip of finest pig. Of meats improperly prepared, one eats too much and pushes to gluttony. Moreover, he is never satisfied and his palate's hunger is forsaken. My sisters I hear your confessions. What is this penchant to stuff yourselves with such ordinary boxes of sugar cakes? You call this sin and you are right, my sisters. Disgusting! For you pollute the temple. I can hear those revolting cakes in your breath. Ladies, how it doesn't avail you! To what does it serve, such sweeties? "The next time," I tell you. "Try a simple éclair with a perfume of chocolate. It is perfect for anyone who sweetooths. It satisfies!"

But Brothers and Sisters it is here that I want to arrive. Because Preparation is all important, the idea comes to me to start a school of Culinary Preparation at the Mission San Martin. I think much about this. It is an excellent project, I am sure, because the natives know to grow the food but practice no art in cooking and so sicken much. They need this Art, brothers and sisters. I tell you. Art is the soul of Soul. And when one eats this Art, it is the highest communion. It is God in the temple! Rejoice!

And so my brothers and sisters, you see of what I think at this moment of Lent. And I am certain you are agree that this school of Culinary Preparation is necessary and an excellent idea. Of course, we must now think of those costs which such a kitchen will need. I did the calculations and have the approximate estimate. I will not tell you it at this time except to say that it rises up quite much. So please give so that this project can be realized. Give now, sooner than possible, if you are alive. I thank you much for your comprehension and giveness. That the Lord Almighty look on you with blessedness. That your heart rest open in this time of the desert.

Pray for me,
Père LeFève

• • •

Easter

Brothers and Sisters,

Christ died, Christ risen, Christ come back! Open your arms to his giveness. How good of him it is! The lamb of God take away the sins of the world. Grant us peace in all the days, in all the ways.

So my friends, how is this Easter time finding you? Prosperity? In good shapes I hope. I thank you for the checks very much. They were provisioned this time, that is to say, all those funds are now in security at the Banco Populario. The School of Culinary Preparation San Martin is not installed but soon we hope so. As you know, the Sisters of the Miraculous Conception reside in the left wing of the Mission San Martin. I tell you, of better neighbors one will not find. I am blessed to have such sisters to my left. How devout and tidy they are! Such angels at work and pray! They inspire one to do good works. They inspire one to serve Him with divine simplicity! This is their way. There is only one thing of which I reproach

168

these consecrated sisters and this is their implication in wisewifery. But a year ago they opened a wisewifery clinique for the native women in this very left wing, where they eat, sleep, and pray. Soeur Bénédicte, who is also from the France, is the chief wisewife and conducts the births with the help of the other good sisters. It is said that she is an excellent wisewife and has never lost child or mother and I do not doubt this. However, it seems to me that this work has a secular taste, most disagreeable. I'm sure that you see as I do. There are doctors at hospital who make these births as a profession. They are men who see many and know many women who birth and are therefore qualified. This is their work. Not so? I cannot but feel that this métier lacks propriety and that the good sisters must occupy themselves with much less fleshy concerns. They are called to drink the blood of Christ, not to soak their hands in the blood of wombs. Now, you must not condemn the sisters because they have a desire to do this work. Their intention is to do Good Works and that in itself is noble. However, they miscalculate their orientation. It is now up to us to re-orient them so that their path is the good one again.

Very soon I do not doubt, you will receive a charity letter from the Miraculous Conception sisters inquiring after funds to build another wing of the wisewifery clinique. This letter will be very dear and sweet to you and you will be touched by the gracious pen of the Soeur Bénédicte. But beware! This pious woman knows not what she does is not to be done in the name of the Holy and Roman Catholic church. I supplicated her and now I supplicate you: Do not send those funds! Instead I pray you to send her letters of disapprobation. Gentle ones, yes. Be sensible. Or if you must to send those funds, send them in care of me, Père LeFève. I believe these good sisters must be discouraged strongly. Not so? You see as I see, I am sure. We are agree. Wouldn't these sisters be better seen in the environs of the School of Culinary Preparation San Martin? I can see them doing good works in the grand kitchen, which, thanks you your giveness, which you must keep up if you're alive!, will be constructed sooner than possible. If all their efforts are made in this kitchen and not in the birthing bed, what a glorious, immaculate institute we shall have indeed! All shall learn to prepare in clean propriety for the sisters are great cleansing ladies. Their aprons will no longer be spattered with womby blood but with dishwasher soaps. But for this, you must to convince Soeur Bénédicte to drop it and interest her in Culinary Preparation. I am the unique voice speaking to her but you are many and can have more successes to persuade her. Not so? Please do so!

Well, my friends, I wish you the most joyous celebration of the resurrection of our Lord and Savior. Remember that in a month, we will too celebrate the ascension of the Blessed Mother into heaven. Remember that each celebration is costly unto the Mission San Martin. Remember that it is because the Virgin *gave* us her son that she rose to the heavens. Remember giveness.

> Happy Easter and pray for me,
> Père LeFève

• • •

Brothers and Sisters,

The Virgin Mary is assumed to the heavens, carried by the angels of God. For this she is somewhat divine, for this she is somewhat risen. Bow your heads my friends and supplicate forgiveness for your sins against the mother. There! She forgives you and pushes you to greater giveness. But if first you don't succeed to have forgiveness, give, give again. After, all shall go well and your conscience refreshed.

My friends, the Soeur Bénédicte just informs me that she is the recipient of many donations and gifts coming from you and perhaps one more sponsorship. She has almost enough of these monies to begin the new wing. Just a few more is necessary. So at this moment I wonder what it was I said to you. Did I not warn you the bad orientation of these good sisters? Did I not supplicate you to dissuade them firmly but well? Did I not ask you to send the monies in care of me? I am terribly disappointed and all the more so that so few funds were sent to the School of Culinary Preparation San Martin's scholarship account. So few my friends! As if no efforts were made at all! Except for the wisewifery which you so heavily subsidized. All this prosperity so that the good sisters continue to occupy themselves with the horrors of accouchement? These virgin sisters are the most pure and gentle of beings, that they could make such angelic cookers if only they did not have this great lie, that wisewifery is holy business. It is not! I beseech you! What is done in hospital is not done in mission. You perhaps pretend that mission works are performed in hospital, such as the dispatching of Eucharist etcetera, but I tell you, the inverse is not possible. It is just as the question of dogs. You do not take your dog into the holy church, the priest's home, but you can be asked to accept the priest's dog into yours. Any question? I think you understand. And so I supplicate you once more, brothers and sisters, to write those letters that will permit the good sisters to turn their hearts near the School of Culinary Preparation and away from the birth bed. Write them sooner than possible. Write them today. Moreover send the monies in care of me, Père LeFève.

Now I speak to you a bit on the School of Culinary Preparation which necessitates more monies than never. I know you say that the costs are cheap because of this native labor which we can pay so little to keep happy. They are so grateful for the smallest of giveness. May the Lord our Savior bless them and give them peace in their day, in all the way! We have offered these jobs of construction to the show-business boys. They are agree to do them. This is for the good, I believe, for the native boys who built the missions of the Padre Junipero Serra, learned soon after to pray in them. So it will be that these boys so amorous of show-business, will learn to prepare delights of culinary exquisite. But it is not the pay, so little, of these show-bizzies that disquiets the Père LeFève, but the costs of material and architect. Must he wait God to shower those monies on him? But God can only shower thanks to you. You are the spout and handle, let his goodness pour through you. Let it pour my friends!

As for architect, I choose a Frenchman, Monsieur Chevier de Chevaucher, a man that knows so much about the cuisine and its necessary goods and tools. He designed the kitchen of Señora Espanoza de Garoso, favorite donor of the Mission San Martin. As you know this lady is of a grand culture and made studies in the France so that she knows the pleasures of the table as they are known there. The Mission San Martin is most honored to invite these two persons into its community, the one as cultivated monies lender, the two as culinary architect. One-half of the sums needed is given to us by Señora Espanoza de Garoso. Now my friends, think of Jesus and of the loaf of bread miracle. From one came much. So it must be with this premier donation. That you make it much and more!

So now, brothers and sisters, my hope is your understanding and giveness. Please! Know this well and open your hearts and checkbooks if you are alive. If not, remember inheritance laws. Give to your church not to your state. Not so? Or this, give to Caesar what is Caesar's but give to San Martin more than the rest. May all of your hearts rise with the Virgin's on this joyous occasion of Assumption.

Pray for me,
Père LeFève.

. . .

Brothers and Sisters

We cannot have a better moment to think about this Mission San Martin than today. For today is the feast day of this holy one upon which this mission was christened. Yes, I speak of Saint Martin the Pilose, patron saint of

Culinary Preparation. What? You say I make a mistake? Not so I assure you. On All the Saints Day, the Roman Catholic church celebrates the communion of saints, all that march in the grand parade. San Martin the Pilose is one of these. There are perhaps other Saint Martins, but this one is known for his protection of the kitchens here and abroad. He is invoked by all who have difficulties in the kitchen and how soon he responds, sooner than possible! When his Holiness the Pope's cook, Massimo Perrini, on the Eve of Vatican Gala II collapsed to his deathbed before having cooked the feast, the invocation of San Martin was made with so feverish efforts, that the cooker rose from this deathbed and cooked the repast, the most splendid than never. This cooker died three days later but was not canonized. For he was not the saint, but the saint was in he. And this saint? San Martin the Pilose, of course, patron saint of Culinary Preparation. So my friends, think not of pleasing me but of pleasing him who watches your kitchen. And you can please him thanks to me, in sending a check to the order of Père LeFève.

Brothers and sisters, I remind you that time is running in! What to do? you ask. Send them, send the monies! If the building doesn't begin in the next month, the building will never begin. The reason for this is because of Vatican fiscality too complicated for writing about here. Just believe me. This is desperate. I also remind you that in the next week, you will have the visit of the Soeur Bénédicte, this mother superior with a big activity in the birthing business. Be careful! She forgets she is in the bad direction for a holy lady and you will too if not careful! She makes many touching photographs of the newborners to show you when she will arrive. You will look at them and surely say, "Why look at those perfect newborners. How nicely the sisters look for them!" But I tell you that these photos are just tricky. The rosy cheeks are made from rouge and their roundness is from the stuffing of cotton balls in the mouths. Without this tricky things, the children are in poor shapes. This is not to say that the sisters don't make a good work. They're doing the best. Only how can we envisage a newborner so poorly nourished to be in good shapes? It is not possible. Remember, a newborner is what his mother eats. So it is a question of sour-milk newborners. Hélàs my friends, you see the problem now, not so? All is in Culinary Preparation! I cannot put enough accents on this case. The sisters of the Miraculous Conception could help better in putting all their funds and prayers in the School of Culinary Preparation San Martin. Think of this when you see the photographs and know that you don't need eyes to believe. Believe me!

Well, my brothers and sisters, I have faith in you good judgments. I have learned you the projects of the Soeur Bénédicte. Beware for how good she seems! And she is goodness only badly oriented. May the angels of God help you with all the burdens and evils. May San Martin the Pilose bless your kitchens.

Pray for me please,
Père LeFève

• • •

Brothers and Sisters,

I write to this advent season with a heart very heavy. A heart so heavy you never know. And for this, I think to return to the France for my retreat. I know that I am not an old man and you say, "Look at him! What great shapes!" But my failures age me more quickly than time. But wait, it is Advent, that we bow our heads one moment and praise the Lord for the arrival of the Savior in Bethlehem. He is the light in this dark winter. That we await his arrival in purple vestments. He is the King of Kings! Hallelujah!

Now, my friends, I tell you what weighs on my downhand heart. It is this: you, my parish, my family, become my traitor. I ask myself truly how this happens? Did I not warn you in the letters? Did I not tell you that the sisters' mission was misplaced? Did I not explain you the necessity of a School of Culinary Preparation? Yes! I did! Not so? Yet the most part of you refused me the monies in favor of the sisters so that in this moment, they build the second wing of the maternity clinic employing the native boys and paying them too many. For all their monies go into showbusiness which is bad business. And now I hear the moaning woman two times more than beforehand. They all push moans two times more and the sisters wave their scissors and cut at the cord. And the blood! To speak of the blood! One prefers to look on a meat to that! Imagine these sisters at the task. Ah! For me it is not possible. And yet it happens so. You are the participants my friends in the creation of something most unholy. I try my friends to offer you forgiveness but this can do nothing to change your giveness. Your giveness is done and not unto me but unto the Soeur Bénédicte. Believe me, I have many tête-à-tête with her for dissuasion but this woman is a true bulldozer. Nothing stops her from her projects. I fear not even papal bull could put the end to this story of second wing. The second wing happens.

And so my projects for the School of Culinary Preparation San Martin fall to the water because your monies never come. Because of Vatican fiscality it is not possible at this moment to remake efforts of donations. I averted you to all of this but you did not heed. It is normal therefore, that I feel deceived. For while knowing my projects you chose the other one, for supporting and donations. Am I not your faithful priest always? My people, my people, why do you forsake me? If nothing else think of malnutrition so common which these natives who know so little of preparation must suffer. Do you feel culpable? My friends you are! Do I forgive you? Good Lord over me I try. Does He forgive you? Repent!

So in this dark winter, my return to the France occupies me. For here all is failed. Except for a miracle from San Martin the Pilose, I do not envisage a longer sojourn at the mission. It is not possible for me to rest here longer although I love it so. May your healths be good in this advent time. He arrives! Pray for me.

Père LeFève

• • •

Brothers and Sisters,

Welcome! Yes, it is me, Père LeFève, here! Encore! You
think I quit the Mission San Martin, not so? Well, not so!
I am in this same moment at the mission so dear. The
France will wait for my older years when my shapes are
not so good. But now I am in full form and stay. Here we
are my friends again at this Christmas time when the
Savior was born into Mary. Hallowed be His name! He
was born of the woman and this birth as well as this
conception beforehand was assisted by the Holy Ghost.
No other virgin bore witness, no other virgin was necessary. Not proof, my friends, that the good sisters' work is
not in birth bed? Let this to the medicine men and to the
Holy Spirit himself. Yes, let it to them. Now, my parish
friends, that we rejoice for the arrival of the Lord. Hallelujah!

My brothers and sisters, I write to you today with the
good news and the bad news. The good news I just stated
above which is my presence ever at the Mission of San
Martin. What joy it is! How I praise the Lord for this good
vein. But the bad news, my friends, chagrins me many and
will you too I am sure. For it is this, that the blessed
Soeur Bénédicte is died just three days ago of a food
empoisonment most terrible. How the poor woman
retched and suffered during the week, only to die on the
Sunday, the X-mas day exactly. The interment was today,
a so desolated moment during which all the persons there
grief with great tears. A pathetic moment, my friends,

indeed. Her casket was flowered with roses by the native women whose starved childrens she helped bring to this world. Look what those children do for her now. No good at all. On this earth she is just a dust. But her soul of course has now peaceful rest in the breast of the Lord.

At this time, I would like to accent how she is died: food empoisonment. Do you see my thoughts? The foods she ate were not prepared correctly. It is a question of bad foods, prepared worse. Did I not warn her? Did I not warn you to warn her? How many natives are died of this empoisonment all the years? Many too many! But such tragedies are escaped with correct preparation of foods. Not so? And so now my friends, I tell you of my definitive decision to transform the second wing into the thing my intentions would like, that is to say, the School of Culinary Preparation San Martin. Are you not agree? So the Soeur Bénédicte was a lady very modest and left great funds not spent in the mission bank account. How lucky we are then. Thanks to this great lady, the school will be built, and a solution to all problem of foods and kitchen will be found.

Yes, I have much idea for this culinary institute. Indeed, much and many more. For example, it is necessary to develop the art of charcuterie. How I wait with impatience to taste the fromage de tête, or, I translate, cheese of head. What delicacy! A dish most distinguished! How it misses here! I will train these native boys to be master charcutiers, to make a cheese of head, crunchy and moist. So one day they will join the Confrérie de Saint Antoine, the Maîtres Charcutiers and wear the white jackets, gloves, and blue royal capes with the pending gold medals. Now this is show-business! Not so? With the blessing of Saint Antoine, this is all possible. Did he not pass his life in the presence of an everlasting sow? Yes he did. The sow followed him everywheres. Ah! My friends, we have so many to do and to prepare. But that we may thank the Soeur Bénédicte, she who passed ahead of us, for her giveness of which we at the School of Culinary Preparation profit so greatly. Thank you, dear sister now in the heavens! San Martin you hear our prayers. How good of you!

Well brothers and sisters, remember that the Mission San Martin is ever grateful for X-mas giveness and fiscal boosters for the new year arrived. May the Lord bless you and grant you peace in this holiday, all the way!

Pray for me (everydays if possible),
Père LeFève

• • •

Fatiha's Bells

*F*atiha was raped as thousands of women before her had been; she was violated behind a fire station. And although she let out screams that could chill a deaf man's spine, not a fireman rose from his slumber to succour her. They slept on in their bunk beds with their hands perhaps tucked between their thighs while the most evil thing was done to Fatiha in the shrubbery. This thing was so evil that Fatiha nearly feared its ending for what would follow, she intuited, could only be more evil still. Yet when she was left alone, battered beneath a rosemary shrub, she realized that the harm was irreparably done, and that she was both spared and ruined. She had known her greatest evil and was yet living. She looked up into the sky, muddied and darkened by a thick fog, and raised her voice to it. "Allah! Is this what you have meant for me? Why then?" But her words had hardly lifted from her when they came back silenced to her throat. Her voice could not carry them, could not take them to the ears of her God. She had lost her way to that communion. Again, she attempted to speak, but her voice seemed to carry nothing forth; it choked and withered. She knew then, truly, what the evil was. Her soul had been stolen by it.

Fatiha tried to get herself up from the firemen's garden and fell back several times for her legs were weak and wouldn't support her. She did not weep but muttered to herself, "Get up! Get up! Get up!" and gripped her dress in a fist. All the while she kept her eye on the sky where the moon should have been. And saw nothing. Eventually she lifted herself up and righted her scarf, which her aggressor had pushed far back off her forehead but hadn't removed. She walked out to the street and down two blocks to her room. And although her legs had not been injured, she walked with an odd and uncertain limp. This was not an affectation but her meager consolation. The limp did not ease the terror in her heart but numbed it there so as to keep it from spreading to the extremities. It tended her getting home. So changed was her countenance that had anyone seen her in the street, they would have guessed her an aged and crippled Muslim woman. She kept her head down, whispering, "Walk along, walk along!" and heard and saw nothing.

When Fatiha got back to her maid's room she did not call the police to report the crime, for she had no phone, nor did she take a bath, for she didn't have a tub. She had only a sink, and after splashing her face with water, she put on her nightgown and lay down. Sleep came to her right away, as a singular offering to the wounded. And that night she wet the bed with sweat. She bathed herself from the inside out and cleaned herself of the man.

The next morning, Fatiha awoke as the late winter sun broke into her window. She opened her eyes, feeling as refreshed and forgetful as she would have any morning. And, as she did every morning before rising, she closed them again for her prayer. This was a ten-word prayer she had recited since childhood by heart-felt rote. It was as essential to her as putting on undergarments before dressing, and yet it wasn't a habit. It was an intimacy. It was a meeting of herself with Herself. It was a morning talk with her god. Yet this morning, the prayer was not there. And when she, most bewildered, tried to conjure it, she could find no conduit to it. The prayer was missing. She opened her eyes then and sat up, believing she would see it before her, but instead her eyes landed on the pile of clothes from the night before. A scream sounded within her, like that of a tomcat screeching at its enemy's odor. She jumped from her bed and began tearing at the clothes with her teeth and hands. She ripped them in a frenzy and nearly lost a tooth doing so. Then she stopped suddenly with a piece of her dress dangling from her mouth and thought of what had happened to her. And once she remembered the event, she remembered the theft. For the event was thievery. "That man who stole my soul has sold his own!" Fatiha shouted in her room. But this thought did not console her as it might have another, for she was a woman who believed in retribution. As for forgiveness, where did it happen, in the heart or in the soul? She could not imagine, for all she felt was a longing for recompense and this desire burned in what was left in her, that is to say in her heart.

Fatiha was a second-year geology student at the University of Paris. Apart from herself and her brother, Ali, who lived in the suburbs, the rest of her family lived in northern Algeria, near the city of Algiers. Fatiha had not been back since she left to pursue her studies in Paris, for the cost of such a trip was not within her means, as she received only a meager stipend from the Algerian government, nor within those of her parents, who had nine other children. However, from time to time she sent them suitcases full of clothes and sundries she collected at the flea markets. She sent them by boat. There was hardly a day when Fatiha did not think of her family, or did not search out items that she suspected might please them. She thought of her family in a bare and loving way; they were as close to her as her own jugular vein. And Allah, she had always been told, was even closer than that. Yet the day after the most evil thing happened to her, her mind did not once turn to the familial home she had left but solely to Allah. To have told her family, even mentally, of her violation would have been, she feared, to put the evil over them as well. Only God, who dwelt more vitally in her, could sustain her. And yet he didn't. Her heart crept up to him all day, but the site where she had always met him was not there. She went to four classes at the university that day and had a cheese sandwich for lunch, which she devoured ravenously, as if she were robbing it rather than eating it. And all the while she never once lifted her head, but kept her eyes on her chest. She was searching her map and eying its geography so as to discern the missing piece. This was how she confirmed what in fact she already knew; what was missing was gone.

That night, Fatiha was not so fortunate with sleep. She was visited by a nemesis who tempted her with the seven downfalls of man, each one more than satisfying her sense of retributive justice. In uneasy dreams she saw herself, abandoned by God and before the rapist, vested with an erupting vengeance. Angry smoke spouted from a fumarole at the top of her head and she shouted, "I burn you! I burn your god!!" Yet when the moment came to prey upon the man, she felt herself not taking a step forward but one backward. She held her scarf over her face and pledged herself to a blue funk. Each time she awoke before the inevitable thing happened, before she saw herself lose her soul again, but only to beat guiltily at her chest for her own cowardice in flinching and not undertaking justice. "N'hargak! N'hargak a-rap dialek! (I burn you! I burn your good god!)," she wailed at the assailant she had closed her dream upon. She tossed and rolled in her bed until the early morning when finally sleep overtook her. However she did not rest long as there was a knock on her door at ten o'clock. It was her landlady's six-year-old daughter, Magali.

"Wake up, Fatiha. You have to go to the market!" the little girl told her from the hallway. Fatiha sat up feeling as if a brick had been hurled at the back of her neck. She rubbed herself, and hearing the girl remembered that she must hurry if she was to do the marketing for her landlord, as indeed she had to do for this was how she earned her keep.

"I'm coming!" she shouted toward the door while getting up. "Tell your mother that I have not forgotten. Put the list under the door." She could hear the girl, Magali, talking to herself and tapping her hands on the banister, then she saw a pink sheet of paper appear from underneath the door. She picked it up and skimmed through it. It was much the same as last week's, only leeks and shallots had been added to it. Fatiha splashed water on her face and dressed hastily. She tied her scarf over her head, grabbed Madame Berger's market basket and rushed down the stairs to the bus stop.

Although Madame Berger, her employer, would not have guessed it, Fatiha did not go to the market down the street, but to another one in the purlieus where she was better assisted and at her ease. It was a thriving, immigrant's quarter where if a man spoke Arabic, he could purchase twenty game hens for the price of five elsewhere. And if a man spoke Swahili, he might dress his wife in boisterous finery for only a pittance of his monthly salary. In this quarter, children were dressed and fed for free. And nobody worried about them but they were cared for by all. Fatiha only went to this neighborhood on Saturdays and although she loved it for the way it reminded her of her home, she never lingered to have a coffee or to sit on a bench on a sunny day. A woman there was supposed to be industrious and to go about her errands. She who wandered or entered the cafés where the men dominated the counters was a free one, or one who lent herself out. Fatiha knew the codes and kept to her business.

However, on that particular Saturday, she did linger after her marketing was done. She stayed longer than she usually did, but with a definite purpose in mind. This purpose had, in fact, been with her since she awoke that morning, although it had only existed then as the seed of an inherited recourse. There was at the market that day, as there was every day, the *taleb*, or witch doctor. He was a small white-haired and bearded man with withered skin the color of an avocado pit. He wore a white turban and sat at a square card table upon which were set three baskets containing different sorts of herbs. His stand was not connected to any of the others but was propitiously placed so that it was sheltered by the awning of a citrus fruit stand. When Fatiha arrived at the witch doctor's, she had to wait a moment for he was with a patient, a middle-aged man wearing a green street-sweeper's jumpsuit. She heard the witch doctor's voice as she stood waiting. He practiced no discretion and seemed insouciant of the personal nature of his client's illness. He spoke loudly so that any passerby could listen in without making the slightest effort. The street sweeper had a pained, embarrassed look and made gestures with his hands for the other to keep his voice down.

"You may tell your wife not to worry. In five days it will be working for you as upon your wedding night. You will have regained your fountain of youth and will use it fruitfully. But I warn you. On the fourth day you will have the hottest urge, but do not appease it. This will only result in a disappointing loss of what has risen. Do you understand?" The man nodded his head to say yes and was given a tiny manila envelope, the kind teeth are sometimes kept in, filled with assorted jujus. He paid, thanked the doctor, and got up sheepishly, without standing up straight. Fatiha did not look his way as he passed by her but went straight to the stand and sat down.

"What's your illness, my sister?" asked the doctor with

his eyes looking down at his baskets. Fatiha could tell by the way he spoke Arabic that he came from the south and was not a Kabyle as his sign claimed. This discrepancy aroused a doubt in her, but she swiftly brushed it aside, for she needed help and had no other recourse.

"I am here," she began, "to get back what was stolen from me. I am here, Brother, to find the soul that was taken from me."

"Then you must go to the person who took it and take it back," said the marabout cavalierly, still not looking at her.

"Fool!" shouted Fatiha, raising her arm and her fist clenched in anger. "Old Fool! You do not know how it was taken! If you did you would not tell me such a cure. I remember nothing of the man! Nothing! Nothing!"

"If it was taken by a man, young sister, I know of your dishonor. And let me tell you. You will be dishonored before you regain it."

"No!" she cried out fiercely. Then calming herself, she began pleading. "I know what you can do. It's so easy. You give me some of those seeds, whatever your science prescribes, and I will sprinkle them on the place I was taken. A week later I will wait there, and the seeds, having worked their magic, will lead my soul back. It's simple, isn't it? I've heard it was done this way. That's all I came for, Brother. Now give me those seeds. I have enough money."

"I tell you, poor girl, that I can offer you no magic of this sort. How many women have come to me for this very thing only to find that justice is hard found! All that I can do for you is help you remember the man. Once you find him, you will have to get it back."

"But how?" asked the girl.

"Bah! How should I know? That's a woman's affair. It's not worthy of men to attempt understanding female trickery. You will do whatever it is you do." The doctor bowed his head and waved his hand above it as if to dismiss her.

"Very well, then. Help me remember," agreed Fatiha. And without saying another word, she waited as he measured and counted the seeds. She paid the fee and left with her tiny envelope of memory herbs.

"A-salama-alicoum," he said to her. "Peace be with you."

"Peace be with you," she said back.

When Fatiha arrived at Madame Berger's apartment on the third floor, the door was wide open. She put down the basket and waited to catch her breath before going in. There were several women in the living room talking at a rather high pitch. She could hear them from the hall.

"When did it happen?" asked one, whose voice she recognized as Madame Berger's.

"Just this morning!" answered another. "He crawled through the bathroom window. It must have been about three A.M. You know her husband's been gone for a week now. He must have known. They say these criminals do their research. Anyway, she was sleeping when he came in. He gagged her mouth and raped her."

"My God! And she's just next door! I didn't hear a thing." Fatiha picked up her bags and walked in, heading straight for the kitchen. The women glanced her way but continued talking. In the kitchen, she began washing the vegetables and fruit. Madame Berger always left her a list that specified the sort of cutting and chopping she needed to have done for that evening's dinner. Fatiha never minded this work and was quite skilled at it; her mother had taught her how to work knives expertly. She opened the cutlery drawer and took out a pairing knife, but before closing it, she let her fingers slide over a cleaver, testing faintly its sharp longitudinal edge. Then, convinced of her need of it, she took it out, wrapped it in an apron, and put it in her coat pocket. When she finished all the kitchen chores on the list, she put a pot of water on the stove to boil for tea, only the tea would be the concoction that would commit her violator to memory. She took the envelope out of her purse and measured the dose for the infusion according to the hand-scribbled instructions the doctor had given her. Then she sat down, exhausted suddenly, and undid the scarf over her head. Her chestnut hair underneath was pulled into a bun, but wisps of hair curled around her temple, giving her a sweet disheveled look. She felt the swell of her thighs on the chair as she planted her feet on the ground. Her lap, at once flaccid and sustaining, was so inviting that even a timid child would not have hesitated to climb upon it. Indeed, the little Magali who had wandered into the kitchen, nestled her head in the Algerian girl's lap and begged to be pulled up onto it. Fatiha set her on her knees and stroked her hair while she sipped at her medicinal drink.

"What are you drinking, Fatiha?" asked the little girl.

"Some tea."

"Can I have some too, Fatiha?"

"No, I don't think so. This isn't good tea for little girls. I'll make you some cocoa."

"No! I don't like cocoa. I want some tea! Give me some, Fatiha. Give me some!"

"Oh, all right then. You can take a sip," acquiesced Fatiha. She held the cup so that the child could drink. She took two sips before she decided it wasn't to her liking.

"It's not sweet, is it, Fatiha?" said Magali, grimacing to show her displeasure.

"No, it's not sweet enough for little girls. Let Fatiha drink it quietly."

The following week, she went about her activities perfunctorily and did not restrain herself from her usual appetites, for she had none. She did not try her chances with Allah; she had given up to her impoverished self. She was waiting. Wednesday night she would babysit Magali and Friday she was invited to her brother, Ali, and his wife, Naima's for dinner. She went to her classes and studied in her room at night. She had neither doubts nor expectations and if one were to tempt her voice with a serinette, one would find one could not entice it. She was stiff and without song. But only because she was expecting so intensely, yes, so intensely that she forgot her hopes. A timepiece ticked within her and she was keeping its count so closely that she couldn't hear its echo. Yet, what her mind could not account for, her body did. Every morning she bathed in her sink and dried herself with a rough, grayish towel. She had no mirror in which to see her body so she perceived it by touch. And her touch was sensing a sharpness, a hardness where before it had felt only welcoming flesh.

She was indeed becoming her own instrument of requital. Everyday, her hand took the cleaver from the previous day's skirt pocket and put it in the one she would wear.

It was Wednesday evening at seven o'clock that she went downstairs to Madame Berger's second-floor apartment. Madame Berger had a date for the evening and had forewarned Fatiha that she might not be back until the next morning. Fatiha brought with her a book and a cosmetics bag. She wore a long, red, satin housedress, a *jepa,* which many Algerian women wore at home or after a bath. It was commodious with two large pockets and three others more surreptitiously sewn in and if need be she could sleep in it. The little girl, Magali, liked to rub her cheek against the smooth sheen of it and would sometimes ask her mother not where Fatiha was but where her dress might be.

Perhaps both Fatiha and Magali were contented to know that they were to be the sole proprietors of their evening. Fatiha excused the girl from her mother's rules, and together they did as they pleased. They sang and played games and let the bedtime hour come as it came. And that night it wasn't until near midnight that the little one yawned.

"Tell me the story of Mr. Congratulations," she said with her eyelids heavy and already closing.

"All right, but first you have to get into bed." She followed Magali into her bedroom and tucked her into bed. Then, gently caressing the little girl's forehead, she began her story.

"Mr. Congratulations, or rather, Mr. Mabrouk, as he is called in Arabic, had two wives, one of whom was in love with her donkey. This happened to be his younger wife whom he secretly preferred, and for this he despaired all the more. The younger wife did her sewing and cooking with the donkey by her side, attached to a rope which she wound around her waist. At night the donkey slept by her side on a bed of hay. She cooed at him sweetly and petted his back. Mr. Congratulations never had a chance to see her as a husband sees his wives. He could only see her with a donkey. Then one day, he decided he had had enough and became very angry with her. 'Either you sell the donkey today at the market or you leave my house!' he shouted at her. The younger wife then, after having done the washing with the older wife, took the donkey and left the house. When she didn't come back that night, Mr. Congratulations grew very worried and admitted to himself that he had done a very foolish thing. He remembered how much he loved her and even cried in the arms of his first wife. He waited three days for her to come back. Then when there was still no sign of her, he left his home in search of her. He told his first wife, 'You've seen a donkey, woman, now help me to look like an ass.' And so the wife began sewing him a suit that resembled an ass. They were both quite pleased with it. Mr. Congratulations put it in a sack and set out to find his wife. He eventually did find her outside of a neighboring village, napping under a tree with the donkey. He quickly put on the donkey suit and walked over to her, doing his best to move like an ass. He knew he would have a better chance at wooing the donkey than at wooing his stubborn little wife. Indeed, he was quite a success! The donkey took to him right away and followed him down the road, despite the wife's pulling at him. Eventually she gave in and followed along, for she could not abandon her love even though he was so ready to abandon her. In this way, Mr. Congratulations led them back to his house and when all three of them crossed its threshold he took off the suit and revealed himself to his wife. 'Ah! Little wife! How I have missed you. It is very good to have you back in our house.' And so all four of them lived together again until one day soon after, when the young wife fell out of love with the donkey. This was no surprise as it is known that a woman can only love an ass for so long. And so it was that Mr. Congratulations got back what had been taken from him by a donkey."

When Fatiha finished the tale, the child was on the brink of sleep and would have certainly surrendered to it, had there not been a noise in the house, a thud.

"What's that?"

"The wind must have blown the kitchen window open. Stay here and try to sleep, I'll be right back. I'm just going to shut it." Fatiha got up, picturing the window flown open and the wind sweeping through as it sometimes did, knocking over the condiments she had left out on the counter. But in the pit of her stomach a dread was warning; it stirred a memory that alerted her body. Even her jaw was not quite right, it quivered, but she would not fathom why. As if independent of herself and of her thoughts, which were dedicated to the window, her hand shut the door to Magali's room behind her. Fatiha walked out into the living room. And while at first glance she did not see the man standing in the corner, she saw him soon enough. She not only saw this man, but she recognized him.

"You!" she shouted. "You! Give it back to me. Give it back to me, what you took!"

"What's that?" mocked the rapist with his hand on his crotch. "You want it? Come here then, come and get it." Fatiha seemed not to register any of this, but, fixed on her own path toward the man, walked on.

"Just give it back to me," she repeated, her voice even and uncompromising.

"Keep coming, little *fatma*, I'll give it to you," he continued in the same derisive tone. He began unbuttoning his pants. Fatiha saw his hands play with the silvery buttons. They were like reachable, glittering stars. Her eyes were riveted upon them. But then, suddenly, something else appeared, the sight of which revealed to Fatiha an immediate horizon, and the impossibility of his rendering anything to her. Clearly there was to be no simple relinquishing. She would have to do the taking this time, before a second theft claimed her. She took one more step toward him and at the same time pulled the cleaver from her pocket. "I burn you! I burn your good god!" she shouted at the man as she raised the knife. The smirk that had been mocking the girl left his face and was replaced by a look of surprised horror. But before he could move back away from her, she gripped him by the waist of his pants and brought the knife down. She heard the sound of tinkling bells. And the man let out a feral cry like that of a mutilated beast. She raised the knife to strike again but the man had freed himself from her grasp and fled from the apartment. And she stood there with her arm still lifted, only recognizing some moments later her own feeling of relief. She dropped her arm and took a deep breath. "I'm glad he is gone," she told herself. "I wouldn't have been able to strike him again." She was strangely convinced of this, that some vital agent of hers would have prevented the second blow. A rustling noise came from the bedroom area which reminded Fatiha that the child must have heard the scream. She rushed to the kitchen and put the knife back in its drawer. Then she went back to pick up what she had cut off, which had fallen to the floor. Just as she was crouching down, Magali came into the room.

"What are you doing, Fatiha? What's wrong? she asked.

"It's nothing, Magali. A gentleman came and dropped all his buttons on the floor. Then, he got scared because they were no longer holding up his pants. He left in a hurry. I'm picking them up now." She cupped several of the buttons in the palm of her hand for the girl to see. Then she put them in a small felt coin purse she kept in her pocket.

"Here," she said, holding the purse out for Magali to take. "They are like bells." Magali took it and wagged it above her head so that it chimed. Fatiha followed her back to her room and tucked her into bed again.

"Tell me the story of Mr. Congratulations."

"Alright," agreed Fatiha. And she began her story of Mr. Congratulations only this time she did not leave out the last words of it as she had before. "Hamdou Lelah," she ended it. "Thanks be to Allah."